BOOKS

w.mascotbooks.com

al to Thrival: Building the Enterprise Startup
The Company Journey

ob Tinker & Tae Hea Nahm. All Rights Reserved. No part of this
on may be reproduced, stored in a retrieval system or transmitted
m by any means electronic, mechanical, or photocopying,
, or otherwise without the permission of the author.

information, please contact:
ooks
don Parkway #320
VA 20170
otbooks.com

e: PBANG0318A
Congress Control Number: 2018900756
78-1-68401-490-3

by Steve Raikow

e United States

SURVIVAL TO THRIV

BUILDING THE
ENTERPRISE START

BOOK 1: THE COMPANY JOURN

m

WWW

Surviv

Book 1

©2018 B
publicati
in any fo
recording

For more
Mascot D
620 Hern
Herndon,
info@mas

CPSIA Co
Library of
ISBN-13: 9

Illustrations

Printed in t

SURVIVAL to THRIVAL

BUILDING THE
ENTERPRISE STARTUP

THE COMPANY JOURNEY

BOB TINKER & TAE HEA NAHM
WITH FERNANDO PIZARRO

DEDICATION

To Christine, Christian, and Chloe, for your love and patience. You made it possible.
—Bob

To Ali, David, and Rosemarie, for your support and being my sounding board.
—Tae Hea

SPECIAL ACKNOWLEDGMENTS

Thank you to the dozens and dozens of entrepreneurs, colleagues, and advisors who helped us along our enterprise startup journey.

Experienced CEOs and Entrepreneurs:
Brett Galloway, Craig Johnson, Faizel Lakhani, Joseph Ansanelli, Mark McLaughlin, Phil Fernandez, Rob Meinhardt, and Yuri Pikover.

2008 First Time CEO Club:
Rob Goldman, Seth Kenvin, and Tien Tzuo

Our Colleagues:
To the entire team at MobileIron for their teamwork and patience with a first time CEO. To the Storm team for sharing your battle scars of company building. And, to our investor colleagues and board members: Aaref Hilaly, Frank Marshall, Gaurav Garg, Jim Tolonen, Matt Howard, and the extended team at Foundation, IVP, Norwest, and Sequoia for your coaching, confidence, and experience.

TABLE OF CONTENTS

SURVIVAL TO THRIVAL:
SERIES INTRO

Entrepreneurship and Silicon Valley have a special ethos: Pay It Forward. Entrepreneurs helping entrepreneurs. Peers helping peers. Colleagues helping colleagues. Experienced entrepreneurs sharing advice and battle scars with new entrepreneurs.

Our journey was made possible by dozens and dozens of people who helped us along the way. From CEOs who were a couple years ahead of us, to previously successful entrepreneurs, to our admittedly awkward 2008 "First-time CEO Club." Just as important were all of our teammates across our startup journeys who brought their entrepreneurial experience and patience to the table.

Every single one of these people, and dozens more, contributed and helped on our journey. Some had a vested interest in our success; most did not and simply helped, often for no reason other than karma and simple thanks. The ethos goes back decades:

> *A 13-year-old Steve Jobs called Bill Hewlett (Hewlett-Packard cofounder and CEO) after finding his phone number in the phone book. "And he picked up the phone, and I talked to him, and I asked him if he'd give me some spare parts for something I was building called a frequency counter, and he did. But in addition to that, he gave me something way more important, he gave me a job that summer...at Hewlett-Packard...and I was in heaven."* [1]

This book is for you, the enterprise entrepreneur

There are few books focused on enterprise entrepreneurs. We decided to tackle that gap and do our part for the entrepreneurial ethos by writing the two *Survival to Thrival* books.

[1] Cupertino Patch newspaper, June 8, 2011

If you are an entrepreneur, an employee, or an investor anywhere on the enterprise startup journey, these books are for you. We've written them to provide big picture frameworks: ways of seeing how things fit together when building an enterprise startup, and how to anticipate what's next; the hard lessons we learned, and then unlearned as the company evolved; a mixture of battle scars on what worked and didn't work for tough situations; things that we saw others do that we wished we had known earlier; and sometimes we just vent about crappy situations for which there is no good answer.

The enterprise: Survival to Thrival

Building an enterprise startup is different. Consumer companies catch a trend just right. They capture zeitgeist in a bottle and accelerate—or they don't, and they're dead. Enterprise companies don't have magical zeitgeist; they're more systematic. Enterprise buyers are more deliberate. Enterprise startups often have more complex go-to-markets. And they often spend way more time in "survival mode," simply trying not to die while they figure out product and go-to-market. Then at some point—if they're one of the lucky ones—the business accelerates. It no longer becomes about *Survival* ("How do we not die?") but about what we call *Thrival* ("How do we win?").

Once an enterprise company accelerates and shifts to Thrival mode, everything changes. What used to work no longer works. Demands on the business change. Demands on the leaders change. Get it right, and the enterprise startup becomes a business that matters and creates enormous value. Get it wrong—fail to evolve, fail to change, fail to make the transition to Thrival—and the startup fades into irrelevancy. That's the enterprise journey, from Survival to Thrival.

Why two books?

Traditional business-book publishers want 200-page books. But today's entrepreneurs consume content in smaller chunks. So, we decided to ignore the publishers and write two smaller books—about 100 pages—that can each be read during a single plane flight.

The first book is about the **enterprise company journey**: lessons learned across the business, product, go-to-market, and team as a startup grows from the Founding Idea, fighting to survive, all the way through to a thriving sustainable industry leader. The book introduces what we believe is the "missing link" to unlock enterprise growth, Go-To-Market Fit, and marks the transition from Survival to Thrival. The changes along enterprise startup journey are both nerve-wracking and breathtaking. Knowing what's coming next is half the battle—as is, ironically, recognizing that what used to work might actually be the exact wrong thing for the next stage. Our hope is that Book One helps entrepreneurs succeed now and anticipate what's next for their company.

The second book is about the **enterprise people journey:** lessons learned—and unlearned—for CEOs, leadership teams, and boards on their journey from Survival to Thrival. As the company changes, roles change, and people must change, or be changed. The startup culture evolves. The way people work together evolves. Some of what makes people wildly successful in the current stage ironically must be unlearned for the next. It is both painfully hard and a spectacular learning experience. Like Book 1, we hope Book 2 helps entrepreneurs succeed now and anticipate what's next, but the focus is on the people and culture rather than the company.

Most importantly, both books have the same goal: to help entrepreneurs who are taking this crazy ride, with all of its ups and downs, recognize that they are not alone.

A little bit about us

The "we" is Bob Tinker, a three-time enterprise entrepreneur, and Tae Hea Nahm (pronounced Tay-Hee Naam), a long-time venture capitalist. We spent the last 15 years on the battlefield together as an entrepreneur-investor combo team, and fortunate enough to help build two enterprise startups from zero to high growth, resulting in one acquisition and one IPO. The first, WiFi company Airespace that was bought by Cisco for $450M, and then mobile security company MobileIron that we took public in 2014.

Bob was the founding CEO of MobileIron, an enterprise startup that, in eight years, went from "three people and a whiteboard" to over $150M in annual revenue, over 12,000 enterprise customers, and nearly 1,000 people. As an executive at Airespace, Bob helped accelerate the go-to-market from zero to an $80M run rate. Like most startup CEOs, Bob doesn't really care all that much about general theories. He wants to charge up the hill, knock down problems, bring the team together, and build a great business. He wants to know how to make good decisions, deal with tough issues, and stay one step ahead. In that sense, he is representative of founder-CEOs, who, unlike investors, are fully committed to a single mission and don't have a portfolio to fall back on. Bob likes to cut to the takeaway for the entrepreneur. He is a punchline guy.

Tae Hea is a founding partner at Storm Ventures. He was an investor in and the chairman of MobileIron, and the founding CEO, investor, and board member of Airespace. Previously, as a founding partner of Venture Law Group, he participated in several hundred startup journeys as an attorney and VC. His work resulted in 15 IPOs. Like many Silicon Valley investors, Tae Hea tends to pattern-match for success and failure across his portfolio of investments. He compares a company situation to his prior experience to understand the drivers that predict future outcomes and help the entrepreneur. As an applied-math major in college, he deliberately (sometimes overly) analyzes the startup journey to create and fit a model. He is a model guy.

Even after 15 years of shared experience, reconciling our two different perspectives to write these books was a surprising challenge. We found the process both painful and fascinating, but hope it delivers a better end result for you. If these books help you better capitalize on your opportunity or avoid even a single pothole, then mission accomplished.

Our wish

Building an enterprise startup is a great ride. A scary ride. And sometimes a lonely ride. In the beginning, it's simply about survival—just trying not to die. With luck and hard work, it becomes about Thrival—your opportunity to build something that matters. No matter what, the journey is an insanely intense learning experience about business, people, and, in the end, yourself. We're all learning every day. For the millions of entrepreneurs around the world who have and will continue to take the plunge to build the next great enterprise company, your journey from Survival to Thrival is an inspiration. Our hats are off to you.

BOOK I:
THE COMPANY JOURNEY

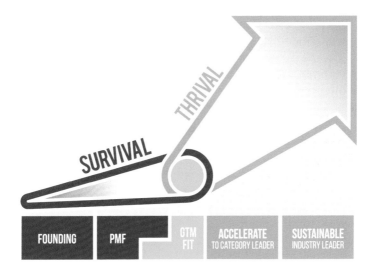

Building an enterprise startup from an idea on a whiteboard into a sustainable industry-leading business is every entrepreneur's dream. This book is about that journey.

Every startup journey goes through distinct stages—from figuring out the Founding Idea and early product, to figuring out Go-To-Market and driving growth, all hoping to build a sustainable valuable business that fulfills the mission. Yet, it's insanely hard. It requires the right idea, the right people, painful setbacks, intense learning—and an immense amount of work and good dose of luck.

Book one's four main themes:

- ***Succeed now and anticipate what's next.*** For enterprise entrepreneurs maniacally focused on their current major startup milestone, practical advice from the battlefield to help win now and anticipate what's next along the path from initial startup idea to sustainable industry leader.

- **The "Missing Link" to unlock enterprise growth: Go-To-Market Fit**. Product-Market Fit is a well-known and incredibly important milestone for enterprise startups, but for enterprise startups, PMF doesn't unlock growth. There is a missing link that doesn't really have an identity, yet it's very real and very important. We call it Go-To-Market Fit.

- **Thrival changes everything:** Once a startup achieves GTM Fit, it's no longer about Survival; it's about Thrival. Everything changes. Execution changes. Mindset changes. Investors change. It's maddening and really hard. Much of what used to work no longer works. The very things that used to work for the startup now hold it back.

- **Damned if you do, damned if you don't:** The enterprise startup journey is fraught with painful situations, difficult changes, and situations for which there is just no good answer. Know that you are not alone.

Enterprise entrepreneurs, this book is for you.

Survive well. Thrive well. Pass it on. Good luck!

Bob & Tae Hea

CHAPTER 1:
FOUNDING

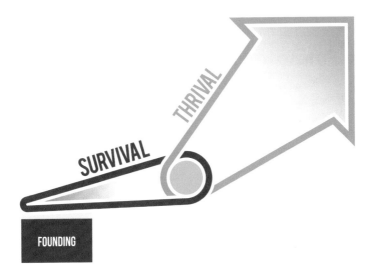

It always starts with an idea.

Some founders see a new product or business opportunity. Others see a major technology or business shift that will disrupt an industry. These founders become enthralled with the opportunity and feel compelled to go after it, no matter the risks. They are natural entrepreneurs—the risk-takers, the believers. They see the huge wave of possibility and promise. They go after it.

Other founders are motivated by personal frustration. Some experience a personal frustration with an unmet problem that causes pain for many companies, and they decide to do something about it. Some are industry insiders who see what needs to happen but are rejected and frustrated by lethargic industry incumbents who are resistant to change. Frustration drives these founders to disrupt the status quo.

And some founders don't generate the original idea. Instead, an idea comes from another founder, a respected advisor, an industry expert or investor—and the idea takes them over. They become converts.

While founders come in all shapes and sizes, they have one thing in common: a Founding Idea. An idea that represents a business or product idea. An idea that solves a customer problem. An idea that can disrupt a market. The Founding Idea inspires passion. The passion to take a risk. The passion to build something from nothing while trying desperately not to die. The passion that it takes to become an enterprise entrepreneur.

The Founding Idea

There are many founding ideas. The challenge is which one of them can become a company that creates value?

Start with a problem or a disruption

Enterprise companies get built on solving a meaningful customer problem or capitalizing on a major disruption. Enterprise customers don't buy technology for technology's sake. They buy to solve problems, improve their business, or defend themselves against disruption.

Starting with the problem may seem obvious, but Silicon Valley often gets it backwards and puts the technology first: "We developed this cool technology. What can we do with it? Let's try sell it to X."

With rare exceptions, this "tech first" approach hurts enterprise entrepreneurs. It can make them invest their time and livelihood on a product that never evolves to address a compelling problem or business need. Even if tech-first approach can raise initial capital, as soon as it fails to gain sales and customer traction, the next round of capital evaporates and the company dies.

Contrast this with the model that puts problems and disruptions first: "We found a painful problem or big disruption that represents a big opportunity for a large set of customers. Let's build a product and solution to capitalize on it, and use some cool technology to differentiate ourselves."

What's different? This approach addresses a clear need—a problem that enterprise customers need to be solved, or a disruption that can create a huge new opportunity. It also establishes a clear product idea, and a clear set of customers. While occasionally a tech-first Founding Idea without a clear customer problem becomes a successful enterprise startup, having a clear problem target and customer target drastically increases the probability of survival, and even Thrival.

Founding Idea: MobileIron

Some founders draw up their Founding Idea on the proverbial cocktail napkin. Bob and the co-founders of MobileIron (Ajay Mishra and Suresh Batchu) did it on a whiteboard.

Disruption Wave:
Smartphones in the workplace

Problem: Employees want smartphones, and to choose their own phone. It is painful for IT to secure and manage that choice

Figure 1: Whiteboard of MobileIron's original Founding Idea

Product: Security and management solution for data and apps on both company-owned and personally owned smartphones

Founding Idea: Do the homework

Founders invest their time and bet their livelihood on their Founding Idea. They do homework to validate the problem, the product idea, the urgency, the market size, and the competitive landscape. And, most importantly, they talk to potential customers: one founder did over 40 customer interviews, and another made over 150 customer calls personally.

Doing the homework comes in many different forms. It can mean talking not only to customers but also to industry experts, existing incumbents, reseller channels, and many others.

> **Bob:** "At MobileIron, my two co-founders, Ajay Mishra and Suresh Batchu, spent six months talking to customers and industry experts before writing a single line of code."

That six months of homework enabled us to understand the customer problem and design a product to solve it, which also made us much more effective raising our first round of capital."

This homework process is critical. Many times, it drives important changes to the Founding Idea. It can provide valuable insight into the urgency of the customer problem and helps crystalize early marketing and positioning. And, finally, it establishes credibility for early investor meetings.

Founding Idea test: Does it have "gravity"?

The ultimate test of a Founding Idea is this: Does it have the "gravity" to attract people and capital?

A great Founding Idea combined with passionate founders creates the gravity. External validation amplifies the gravitational force. Validation can come from credible customer discussions. Validation can come from credible third parties. Validation can come via an illustrative prototype. Validation via an initial working product is now increasingly feasible for enterprise startups thanks to cloud infrastructure services that simplify development. The best validation of all is through early enterprise customer traction, either paid or unpaid.

For team members, gravity is created by tackling a meaningful problem with a compelling solution, working with great people, capitalizing on a transformational wave, and building a great company. For investors, gravity is created by the belief that the market wave is large enough, that the startup can enter the market and gain a defendable foothold, and that the problem has enough urgency to drive customers to buy sooner rather than later.

When the gravity of a Founding Idea brings together people and capital, something special happens. The Founding Idea takes on a life of its own. The critical mass of the Founding Idea, people, capital, and customer validation come together to light a spark inside the team. The team begins to emotionally attach to the Founding Idea and the problem it solves for customers. The team begins to feel part of a larger cause. The mission is born.

The co-founders

Co-founders are the seed corn of the startup. They develop the Founding Idea. They recruit the early team. They set the company culture. They raise the initial investor capital. Picking the right co-founders can accelerate an enterprise startup and cement investor backing. Picking the wrong ones (or too many) can severely damage an enterprise startup.

How to think about building a founding team? What do they have to do? What are the problems they are likely to face?

Co-founder fit

Before looking at co-founder skills, the most important aspect of co-founders is fit. This boils down to three things:

- **Passion.** A shared passion for the mission and Founding Idea.
- **Chemistry.** A solid working relationship. Comfortable spending a *lot* of time together. Similar risk tolerance and commitment level.
- **Trust.** Shared values. Can depend on one another.

Co-founder skills

Co-founders shouldn't all have the same backgrounds and skills. The best founding teams bring together a mix of skills, which allows a startup to move from its founding idea to a paying product or service. Ideally, the mix includes people who can take responsibility for:

- **Product.** Understand the problem and solve it with something that can sell.
- **Technical.** Build the product.

- **Sales and Marketing.** Find customers and sell the product.

This doesn't mean a team always needs three co-founders, one for each of these categories. Early on, a CEO can sometimes play multiple roles—finding customers, defining requirements, selling—while a CTO builds the product. Or a CEO can find customers and sell while a CTO works with customers to define requirements and build the product. What matters is that the team has the needed skills. Over time, as the startup grows, the founders' roles will narrow. Ideally, co-founders have the capability not only to get the company started in early stages but also to play leadership roles in future stages.

Note that co-founders do not have to form a complete team. Many times, other team members (such as a great VP Sales or VP Customer Success) are easier to recruit at the next stage of the company journey. Some startups mistakenly hire "execs" early, which leads to one of the main founder challenges: too many co-founders (See Founder Challenge #1).

Founders set the culture

If product is a company's muscle, and the founding team is its brain, then culture is its soul.

Founders set the company culture. They make up the early executive team and they set the pace for execution. They provide guidance and inspiration to new hires. And remember: by the time a startup hires its first 20 people, the culture is set.

The founders therefore have a choice: (1) Be proactive about how to set and build the culture, or (2) Let the culture evolve organically. Both are fine. The key is to pick one consciously. We talk about this in greater detail in Book Two of this series (*Survival to Thrival: The People Journey*). Founders and the startup culture are deeply intertwined.

The founder oath: Separate mission and ego

Passion and commitment are what make a great company, but they can also have some damaging side effects as companies evolve, especially when founders hold onto their role beyond what is best for the mission. Because of that, founding teams have to have a mature conversation early on about how everyone on the team, including the CEO, will at some point probably need to step aside—especially if the company is successful. It's about the mission, not the person. That makes perfect sense—until you're the one who has to step aside from a role that you've poured your heart and soul into for years. It's really, really hard. But it's also necessary.

> **Bob:** *"At some point in MobileIron's growth, every one of us had to step aside from our founding roles. It didn't feel great. It was awkward and weird. But it was the right thing to do—for the mission and for the hundreds of employees and their families who had bet on it. Nothing can screw up a great startup faster than founder drama, where egos get in the way of the mission. I'd love to see all founders take a Founder Oath."*

It's about the Mission, not the Person

- *I <state your name> promise that my company is about the mission <insert mission here>, and not about me.*
- *I promise to do my best to separate my ego from the business.*
- *I recognize few things can screw up a great company as much as founder drama.*
- *If at some point the company is fortunate enough to grow beyond me, I will gracefully step aside and set the team up for success.*

Ideally, some or all of the founders will be able to adapt and grow as the company evolves and leadership roles change. In reality, though, this doesn't always happen. Sometimes a company's needs to extend beyond a founder's ability to serve as a functional executive. That's normal, and totally okay. The important thing is to respect that person's historical contribution to the company and respectfully help them either find a productive new role in the company or move on to their next mission.

Founder challenge #1: Too many co-founders

Some startups fall prey to the too-many-founders syndrome. This can create both short-term and long-term problems. There's a clear right and wrong here: fewer co-founders is better than more.

In the early stages of an enterprise startup, co-founders make numerous major directional decisions that impact the fate of the startup. Having too many co-founders complicates decision-making. Too many co-founders makes determining equity ownership for founders more complex. Too many co-founders can drive a company to do organizational gymnastics to place people who have a co-founder title in meaningful roles. Too many co-founders often means some founders have a lighter workload than others, which can lead to resentment among the other founders and the rest of the team. This, in turn, can lead to founder instability and conflict over equity ownership.

The decision to add a co-founder is a serious decision. Before adding a co-founder, ask these questions: Does the person have founder fit? If so, does the person bring a needed capability to the startup that justifies adding a founder right now? Could an existing founder or key advisers do it instead, at least for now? If the answer to that last question is yes, you'll probably be better off not making that person a co-founder, and instead hiring them (or somebody else) later as an executive.

Founder challenge #2: The equity split

How do founders split equity? This is a financial question—and an emotional one. Every situation is different, and no amount of data and comparables will get you past that. Founders will have different views of fairness, of their contribution to the Founding Idea, of the value they bring, of prior relationships, of timing, alternatives, and so on. It's difficult to capture those elements all at once. The resolution of this question is specific to each founding team with many outcomes along a possible spectrum. (See the following chart.)

Examples with 4 Co-Founders

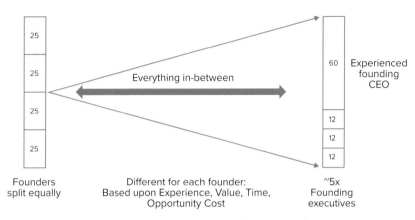

Figure 2: Equity Split Ranges with 4 Co-founders

On the left end of the spectrum, every founder is the same, and the founders split equally. On the right end of the spectrum, one founder, usually a proven founder-CEO, gets the largest share, with other founders divvying up the remainder.

At the right end of the spectrum, a common ratio for the equity given to an executive and the CEO is 1:5, which can be less if the founder is not likely to be a long-term executive.

The hard part is that most founder situations fall somewhere in-between. Different founders bring different value and experience to a startup. Different founders forego different opportunities to join the founding team. All of that has to be factored in. And it has to be done in a way that makes sense to everybody. In some cases, a useful tool to bridge gaps is to create future equity grants for founders that are tied to specific business outcomes, such as product delivery or customer targets. But the bottom line is that determining founder equity is always tricky—and very personal.

Tae Hea: "The founder-split decision has a surprisingly long half-life inside a company. In several companies, co-founders raised the 'unfairness' of the original split many years after the company's founding, and after many refresh grants. I've learned that the founder equity split is more than economics. For the founders, it conveys a message about personal value."

Founder challenge #3: Founder drama

For co-founders, embarking on a start-up is like getting married, often without much dating. The challenge, unfortunately, is that sometimes co-founders only later realize they don't work well together, often resulting in bitter founder drama. Employees are forced to take sides. Decisions are paralyzed. Culture is damaged. It's like a divorce that creates collateral damage to the company, employees, and investors. Some common reasons for founder drama:

- The founders don't agree on the vision, direction, values, or culture. Even the smallest disagreements are magnified in the very high-stress world of an early-stage startup.

- It's not clear who the CEO is. Early founder leadership roles are fluid. Sometimes a non-CEO founder raised most of the early capital. But in the end, there needs to be one CEO who can make final decisions. Lack of clarity or latent resentment about who is CEO creates toxic politics.

- One co-founder is perceived as not contributing or working to the same level as the other co-founders. Everybody has to carry their weight.

- The co-founders disagree about equity allocations. After raising capital and allocating equity for employees, the remaining equity is sometimes not enough to satisfy every founder. This problem is magnified if there are disagreements on the prior three reasons.

Founder drama can exasperate employees and investors and make them give up. Founder drama can quickly kill a startup. Some companies can survive founder drama if they have CEOs and boards who act quickly and decisively in response, but the best approach to founder drama is to prevent it from happening in the first place. That means thinking hard *before* making somebody a co-founder. Carefully consider what it will be like to work with that founder candidate, and the candidate's fit with the ground rules on vision, values, culture, equity, and lines of authority.

The pioneering team: Choose wisely to survive

Founders and the first employees are the pioneering team, embarking on a mission to build a company from nothing. The early team is the foundation of a company's culture and its ability to succeed. Skills matter. Chemistry matters. Passion matters. Luck matters.

The romantic view: the early team is embarking on an exhilarating ride that will make their startup into a thriving business. The practical view: they're going to have to work their tails off to survive, win customers, resolve conflicts under intense pressure, and achieve milestones that justify new rounds of capital. The bottom line: in the early days, a founding team will go through some of its highest highs and lowest lows.

The mission for the early team is simple: survive long enough to exit founding stage with a Founding Idea that has enough validation and proof points that attracts people and investor capital. Basically, create gravity.

Then drive to the next milestone: finding Product-Market Fit, or PMF (the subject of the next chapter). The early team is small—capital is scarce and every penny matters. Early hires should have specific technical customer, or market skills. The team must simultaneously balance the idealistic passion for the mission of the company with practical month-to-month survival.

The early investors: Pick like a co-founder

From the founders' perspective, picking an early-stage investor (especially the lead investor, who will serve on the board) is like picking a co-founder. For the investor, placing a bet on a yet-proven Founding Idea requires a leap of faith—the same leap that a co-founder has to take. Belief matters: belief in the Founding Idea, and belief in the founding team. Fit matters: fit with the co-founders, fit with the market, fit with the risk. Trust matters: a solid relationship marked by trust and candor buttresses a startup when the inevitable ups and downs start to put stress on the company. An early investor should contribute not only just capital but also expertise and relationships to help the company exit founding stage, achieve Product-Market Fit, and move beyond.

Be prepared for an unpleasant side effect of finding the right early investor. Other than unusual circumstances, finding the right early investor takes time and meeting different investors. Unfortunately, those meetings often educate the investment community and can accelerate funding of potential competitors. Discretion is useful, but being overly secretive is rarely effective. Execution is what matters in the end: the company that executes better will win.

Founding path is non-linear and uncomfortable

To get through the founding stage, a startup needs to refine the Founding Idea, recruit the founding team, hire key advisors, raise the initial funding, meet the target customers, define the product, and start developing the product. All these deliverables are important. All are necessary. All are interrelated. But what sequence to do them in? Which one should come first?

First-time founders (especially those with strong execution backgrounds) crave a linear path or process through the founding stage. It usually doesn't work that way. The path tends to be a non-linear mix of planning and opportunism.

Organized customer interviews help refine the Founding Idea. But an introduction to a key advisor or customer can also drive major changes in the idea. Networking to find early employees and investors is both deliberate and serendipitous. An opportunistic meeting with a potential advisor could lead to the ideal teaching customer, who helps refine the product requirements, which together leads to the initial funding, which then leads to the first hire. Founders have to shift their energy from focus area to focus area in order to learn, fill in gaps, and achieve early deliverables. Maybe they spend a day building a prototype. Then a day doing customer interviews. A day networking. A day meeting investors. A day completely re-thinking an approach. Founders have to know that what they do today can often be quite different from yesterday or tomorrow. The path through the founding stage often lacks clear definition, but what's necessary to exit the founding stage is usually clear: the ability to raise capital and shift gears to iterate to product-market fit.

Think ahead: Milestones to make the next round easy

Once a startup has finished the founding stage and raised capital, what's next? There are so many things to do. What should the founders prioritize?

The answer is this: At the beginning of each stage, establish key business milestones that will allow you to easily make your next financing round at roughly a 2x valuation—and then survive on your existing cash until you hit those milestones.

These milestones are usually a mix of product and customer traction, combined with some sort of market proof. They become a unifying set of goals for the team to execute against. For example, a company might strive to get five paying reference customers for a live product, or to achieve an active user base of X with a sales pipeline of $X.

> *Tae Hea: "It is not unusual to see a team who believes that they have made a huge amount of progress—yet can't raise additional funding and have to shut down. Every startup should have a clear understanding of the specific milestones required for an easy next round."*

Creating overly complex milestones with false levels of precision doesn't help. Sometimes, first-time founders—particularly those who have been executives at large companies—start with an overly detailed three–five year execution plan that looks impressive but becomes immediately outdated when it collides with the reality of building a startup.

Better are simple milestones that everyone can understand and that justify the next round. Coming up with these milestones is harder that it sounds. And for the startup team, delivering against them takes a crazy amount of hard work and, as always, a dose of good luck.

PUNCHLINES

» Founding Ideas and teams must create gravity to attract people and capital.

» Start with a problem or a disruption, rather than a technology. Enterprise customers don't buy technology for technology's sake. Do the homework to validate the Founding Idea with customers.

» Picking the right co-founders is a mix of fit and skills. Founders should bring different skills to the table. Minimize the number of co-founders. Founders and early team define the culture and the work ethic.

» Take the Founder Oath: Separate mission from ego. Founders holding on too tight creates drama and holds back the company. Have a mature conversation in the beginning.

» Pick early investors as you would pick co-founders.

» The path through founding stage is a non-linear mix of planning and opportunism.

» At the end of each stage, plan ahead by setting milestones to make the next round of financing easy.

CHAPTER 2:
PRODUCT-MARKET FIT

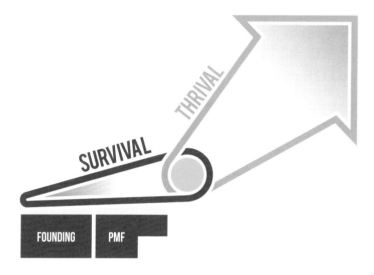

The enterprise startup has a Founding Idea, a founding team, and enough gravity to attract people and capital. Now the team must work their tails off to get from that idea to a product that customers will buy. The founding team will build and iterate constantly on the product and the Founding Idea—and then iterate and build some more. They'll find early customers and make key early hires. They'll get feedback from every direction. It will be noisy and chaotic. So what's the measure of success at this stage? Is it the number of sleepless nights? Lines of code? Product requirements met? Happy investors?

No.

Introducing Product-Market Fit

The measure of success during this phase is achieving Product-Market Fit (PMF).

PMF is a critical milestone and a well-documented concept. Lots of great articles defining PMF and how to find it have been written for entrepreneurs. But they primarily focus on PMF for consumer startups. Instead, we're going to cover what's different about PMF for enterprise startups, and the particular challenges that entrepreneurs confront in trying to find it.

Teaser for Chapter 3: While PMF is a hugely important milestone for the enterprise startup, PMF alone is not sufficient to unlock growth.

PMF for enterprise startups: It's different

Paying reference customers

In the consumer world, PMF is often defined by adoption or usage. Enterprise PMF is different.

Enterprise PMF isn't just about adoption and usage. It's also about *paying reference customers.* That is, good customers who (1) pay you money, (2) actively use your product, and (3) are willing to recommend you to others. Paying reference customers are the essence of enterprise PMF.

There are some exceptions to this rule. It doesn't apply, for example, to enterprise startups that are following a "freemium-and-upsell model," where early adoption doesn't necessarily mean customer payment. However, even with freemium-and-upsell model, PMF involves validating the startup's ability to convert from free to paid.

How do you know?

Deciding if the enterprise startup has achieved PMF can be confusing because of the number of different signals coming from customers, the market, and the team. How do you know?

Bob: *"The thing we figured out is that the founders and the product team don't decide PMF. The customers and the sales team decide. When it happens, you can see it and feel it. Customers are willing to give you money. Customers spend their valuable time with you and your product.*

Sales reps see an improvement in getting customers to second meetings. Customer feature requests pile in as customers operationalize your product."

A classic mistake is to declare PMF after hitting some product-focused milestones and landing a couple of trial customers. Product teams don't decide PMF. Customers decide PMF. They vote with their money and their time.

There are three specific signs of enterprise PMF:

- **Paying Customers.** This is a huge signal of success. To put this in perspective, the sponsors inside early customers had to put their necks on the line and tell their bosses, "I want to buy this new product from some new little company that you've never heard of and may not be around in 2 years."

- **Real usage.** Paying customers by itself is not enough. What matters in the end is that customers use the product in operational situations where business processes depend on it. Ironically, loud customer complaints when product issues happen is a sign of importance (but better to avoid issues).

- **Recommendation/Virality.** Customers start recommending the product to their peers, and inbound customer interest accelerate.

Finding PMF: The path through the woods

Finding PMF resembles a pioneer searching for a path through the woods. It involves starting with a Founding Idea. Constantly listen, iterate, and improve the product and the idea. Rarely does the Founding Idea and product conception perfectly survive contact with the real world of customers. Be open to adjacencies that could uncover a customer hotspot of pain and demand, but not so many adjacencies to be unfocused. Then, with hard work and luck, converge on the customer hotspots that achieve PMF. Finding the path through the woods is an intense, noisy, scary experience that is a mix of structured analysis, iteration, exploration, and good old-fashioned customer-product intuition.

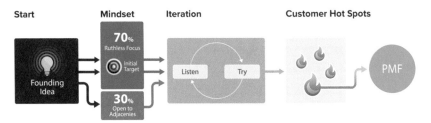

Figure 3: Path from Founding Idea to Product-Market Fit

Start with the product-market hypothesis

To find PMF, start with the hypothesis of a compelling solution (the product) to a huge pain point experienced by a specific customer segment (the market). Working with that hypothesis, do three important things:

- Find customers who fit the target
- Iterate on minimum viable product
- Validate customer interest.

Focus but be open to adjacencies—even if that seems like heresy

Some startups (especially those with passionate founders) make the founding product-market hypothesis their exclusive focus. Focus is a great thing, but religiously keeping it narrow is a high-risk approach. That's because the founding product-market hypothesis rarely survives intact after contact with the real world. Often a slightly different customer segment, or an adjacent pain point, turns out to be a more compelling "hotspot" and PMF opportunity.

Start with the initial focus on the product-market hypothesis, but also cast a slightly wider net for adjacent pain points and customer segments.

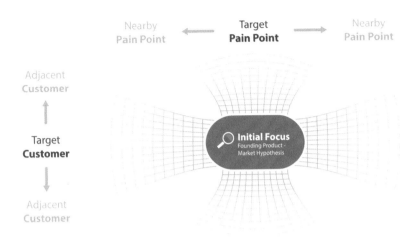

Figure 4: Cast a slightly wider net into adjacent
pain points and customer segments

Targeting product-market adjacencies isn't free. Testing them diverts resources from the original idea. There is no hard-and-fast rule on this, but spending 20–30 percent of your energy testing adjacencies provides enough coverage to detect a potential hotspot that may be outside the initial focus. Ask customers "what other problems are you struggling with?" Deliberately meet customers in different segments. Ask probing questions "if we had such-and-such, what would that mean to you?". Modify initial pitch decks to catalyze exploratory discussions. Be willing to test adjacencies with digital marketing, prototypes or mockups. Testing adjacencies also complicates early sales calls, because they won't be identical and will require some nimbleness. Emotionally, too, this approach can be difficult for founders and first developers, since by definition they are passionate believers in the Founding Idea. Pursuing anything else can seem like heresy!

Critical but unsung skill: Gathering customer data

Gathering the right customer data is a real skill. First is collecting unfiltered data:

> **Tae Hea:** "Our founder has a unique gift for building relationships with potential customers and collecting valuable unfiltered data. He wouldn't filter the data to fit his original product-market hypothesis. We heard what

customers were really saying. With his input, we pivoted away from the original hypothesis and found a different hotspot, which got us to PMF."

Second is collecting customer data in a structured format that will accelerate the analysis. Start with a common framework and list of questions to gather comparable information that eliminates bias. Refine the data framework and questions over time to focus on the most important information for the startup.

Customer interviews: seek ruthless feedback and "teaching customers"

The first customer meetings typically are with "friendly" potential customers who are already known by the founders or are introduced by a mutual connection (e.g., advisors, investors). While these potential customers provide detailed and honest feedback, their historical relationships to the team may include some bias.

Customer interviews must go beyond friendly customers. Find customers that represent the target segment. Seek out ruthless feedback. And, keep an eye out in particular for "teaching customers." What are teaching customers? Thoughtful potential customers who have both vision (a view of the future world) and practicality (a view of what's useful and would be bought) to help you iterate during PMF.

Digital marketing as a test bed

Digital-marketing methods, like search advertising and email campaigns, can help test early customer interest and gather early customer feedback before the early product is even ready.

To test early customer interest, try using paid search advertising around different pain points, and measure the response. Or try using paid search ads to drive traffic to landing pages that describe different versions of the solution, and measure the response. Send emails to different potential target customers with different descriptions of the pain point and solution, and measure the responses and actions, such as opens, clicks, downloads, and registrations.

Digital marketing's ability to systematically test pain points, solution descriptions, and target customers at scale serves as an effective complement to direct customer interviews. Digital marketing importantly enables startups to gather feedback from potential customers who are not known through prior relationships.

> **Tae Hea:** *"One CEO excelled at sales and digital marketing, but was not a developer who could prototype. Instead, he tested potential product-market fit ideas through website and content marketing ahead of product development. The marketing and website results, plus follow-up phone calls, highlighted a more attractive adjacent hotspot. He pivoted the company and achieved Product-Market Fit."*

Nailing PMF: Listen and iterate to 20 paying customers

Getting to 20 paying customers and finding PMF isn't a linear process; it's cyclical. First you listen. Then you make changes. Then you listen some more. It's constant iteration until you find the set of features that fits the pain point.

Why 20 paying customers? We picked that number. The right number for your startup could be more or less. The key is to pick a number of paying customers that represents a meaningful number of customers with a common problem for which your product represents the right solution—and those customers are willing to pay for it.

The path to 20 paying customers is noisy. Deals are moving in and out of the sales pipeline. Different customers have slightly different problems or views of the right solution. Lots of people inside the startup are naturally talking directly to customers. The challenge is not getting enough customer feedback but often getting too much, and then sifting through it. Getting structured customer feedback really helps the analysis. Evaluating this early feedback can be a source of contention in an early-stage company—especially if the feedback suggests that the company needs to pivot away from its founding product-market hypothesis.

- **Watch out for confirmation bias.** It's dangerous only to listen to feedback that confirms the initial hypothesis. Ironically, this is a bigger risk for experienced or passionate founders.

- **Customers know best.** Overweighting the opinion of a VC board member can send a company down the wrong path. The VC doesn't buy the product. Customers do. And data trumps opinion.

Picking the PMF hotspot: Often harder than it looks

With a too-narrow focus on the core target, a company may only get four or five paying customers and miss a hotspot in a nearby adjacency.

Picking your hotspot can be tricky. What are the clusters where you feel real traction? Which cluster has a future that you can depend on? Which cluster comes with urgency? Often one or two clusters become your PMF hotspot candidates. Focus on those hotspots and drill in: iterate, improve, and work like fiends to win those first 20 customers.

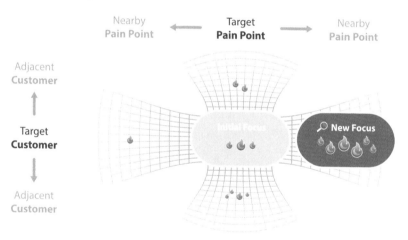

Figure 5: Find the customer hotspot where the cluster of customers and pain intensity means opportunity

Tae Hea: *"Early on, EchoSign, an electronic documents signature SaaS company, had several legitimate use cases that formed hotspots: HR offers, internal approvals, sales contracts, and document management. They were all legitimate candidates with real customer opportunities. But one use case was the hotspot with the most traction and felt like it had the deepest pool of customer opportunities: using EchoSign to help sales* *reps speed up customer signatures on sales contracts. The team zeroed-in on the sales contract hotspot, and found PMF."*

Narrowing down on the hotspot is harder than it sounds for two reasons. First, picking the right hotspot will be a mixture of current information, market data, and educated guesswork. And second, narrowing to a single hotspot means the enterprise startup in Survival mode must painfully say no to very legitimate near-term revenue opportunities outside the selected hotspot.

MobileIron: Adjusts and Finds PMF

MobileIron's PMF was different than the initial founding hypothesis. Two adjacent hotspots turned out to be the compelling opportunity and catalyzed PMF. If MobileIron had stayed dogmatically focused on the initial hypothesis, the company would have missed a much larger opportunity and perhaps never have found PMF.

MobileIron's initial founding hypothesis: Smartphones (primarily Windows and Nokia) are computers. Provide security, management, and expense-reduction so that enterprise companies can adopt smartphones and control costs.

Adjacent hotspots: As it turned out, two adjacent hot spots became much more compelling for enterprise customers: (1) iPhone security for email and mobile apps. (2) Enable BYOD (Bring Your Own Device) to work which separates personal and work information.

Bob: "Finding our adjacent hotspots was partly listening and paying attention to adjacencies—and part luck. We started MobileIron in 2007, the same year Apple launched the iPhone. Over the course of 2008 and 2009, the iPhone was dragged into the enterprise by users— some were owned by the company, some were owned by employees. IT Departments were both struggling and curious about the opportunity. So we took a risk and ex-

perimented on an adjacency. Our original iPhone-centric product designs were sketched out on Post-It notes.

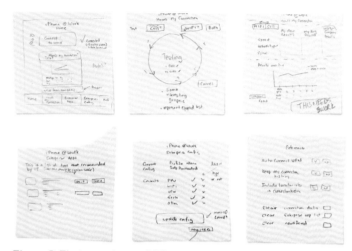

Figure 6: First experimental iPhone product design on Post-It notes

Some felt this experiment was an unnecessary distraction from our core original focus. Yet as we iterated and tried it with customers, we were able to get first meetings more quickly. Customers wanted to test the functionality. We started getting inbound calls as customers talked to each other. We knew this was it—we had found our hotspot for PMF, and we never looked back."

Engagio: Fast path to PMF & $1M Annual Recurring Revenue in 15 months

Engagio is a SaaS provider of Account Based Marketing software and led by a repeat entrepreneur. Engagio's founding CEO, Jon Miller, was previously a co-founder of Marketo. Engagio went from 0 to $1M ARR in 15 months, which was very fast. Don't despair if it takes longer. The table below shows Engagio's timeline, along with the key milestones and sequencing.

Figure 7: Engagio timeline from $0 to $1M in ARR

- **Hired one complementary co-founder.** Jon had experience in product, marketing, and sales.
So, Jon recruited a single co-founder with strong technical skills.

- **Did the customer homework:** Jon developed a crisp understanding of the customers' pain point by personally making all the early customer calls, validating the early product with more than 100 sales demos—all before hiring the first sales rep.

- **Raised capital:** Armed with customer validation, Engagio closed Series A to fund this plan.

- **Iterated to minimum value proposition while painting vision of future:** To deliver value quickly and speed adoption, the initial product was an add-on to an existing third-party platform (Salesforce). The company then rapidly improved that simple product while simultaneously painting a roadmap to a thought-leading destination. Progress against the roadmap and the thought leadership convinced early customers to bet on Engagio.

- **Found Product-Market Fit:** Engagio achieved PMF by iterating on product and measured success by passionate customers who loved the product and used it daily.

- **Generated leads and thought leadership:** Even in its early days, the company generated many qualified leads via thought leadership. A book on Account Based Marketing generated 1500 downloads and over 120 demo requests in just a couple of months, plus numerous speaking events and webinars.

- **GTM team hiring sequence:** Instead of first hiring a VP of Sales, Jon's first GTM hire was a VP Customer Success along with the first beta customer. At 25 paid customers, Jon hired two sales reps. Only after proving success with the two reps, did Jon hire a VP of Sales.

PMF challenges

Overcoming founder bias

The hotspot that leads to PMF may not be exactly the one in your initial hypothesis. That's okay and normal. So is the feeling that testing an adjacency is at best distracting and at worst like ideological heresy. Do it anyway. Finding PMF and company survival depends on it.

When PMF feels elusive

Sometimes PMF feels elusive. PMF requires a combination of solving real customer pain coupled with meaningful usage to generate paying reference customers. PMF problems often occur when either pain (business value) or usage are insufficient or misaligned.

Is the customer pain urgent enough to drive meaningful usage? This may be a fundamental market issue. Is actual customer usage of the product surprisingly unrelated to the pain for which the product was originally sold? That may be a clue to a valid adjacency. Is the pain high enough, but usage low? That is likely a product insufficiency. Or it could be the unusual case where it's a high pain problem that occurs infrequently, therefore value is intermittent. These are market and product issues that may or may not be solvable.

Another source of PMF elusiveness is internal misalignment. One team is trying to market and sell a pain or business value that gets customer attention, while others are driving product usage for a different use case without enough pain relief to trigger a sale and remain sticky. These are organizational issues that are solvable. In either case, the key to PMF is solving a material pain that drives sufficient usage of the startup's product to create business value for the customer.

Some early customers get left behind

As you iterate toward PMF, some early customers likely bought your product for a value proposition that ends up outside your eventual hotspot focus area. What happens to them? They get left behind. Customers who went out on a limb to bet on your product are now stranded. It's painful.

> **Bob:** "We had one early customer, a pharmaceutical services firm in North Carolina, who bought our product for a set of features that we subsequently chose deprecate. They were ticked, and rightfully so—they had paid us. We flew to meet them, apologized, explained the situation, and handed them a check refunding their money. Two years later, they bought our mainline product, and became a long-time customer."

PMF side-effect: Technical debt

Technical debt is result of product or technical shortcuts taken during the fast-product iterations in search of PMF. Early tech debt is virtually unavoidable. Tech debt is often a "damned-if-you-do, damned-if-you-don't" problem.

Tech debt stinks. Tech debt slows down development and creates quality issues. Refactoring to solve tech debt is a painful resource distraction. Yet, both are a reality in most startups. Why? Tech debt is a natural byproduct of iterations to PMF. If a startup pursues perfection by building the perfect original product, it will be late to market, never find PMF, run out of cash, and die quickly. Alternatively, if after finding PMF with the experimental features, the startup accelerates development without repaying the tech debt, the startup can die slowly. It's a balance. Tech debt only really matters if the startup is successful enough to make the shift from Survival mode to Thrival mode—which is a good problem to have.

What is tech debt? Huan Ho, a co-founder and CTO of RallyTeam, describes the creation and resolution of technical debt with the steak knife to Swiss Army knife to Samurai sword diagram below.

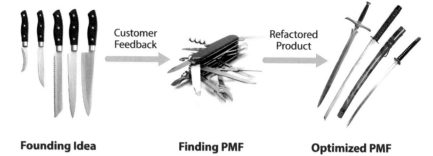

| Founding Idea | Finding PMF | Optimized PMF |

Figure 8: Tech debt is like a Swiss Army knife

The Founding Idea is a set of steak knives, a clean well-defined product. In the search for PMF, customers provide diverse feedback, each wanting various knife modifications to fit their need. Anxious to find PMF and win early deals, the company iterates quickly, building different types of knives. Then great news: the company found PMF with one of the knives, in this case a very sharp long sword for Samurai's. The bad news: PMF-winning the Samurai sword is embedded in a Swiss Army knife. The extraneous knives and unneeded complexity resulting from iteration is technical debt. Technical debt negatively impacts scalability and increases complexity that slows down development. Technical debt in the form of legacy unused features or architecture decisions become quality landmines as production scales. How to solve this technical debt? Gradually refactor the Swiss Army knife to be optimized as a Samurai sword.

Advice for tech debt

- Hire an overqualified early engineering team (if you can!) for the first developers. Good engineers know how to make things solid and where shortcuts can be taken.

- Keep a list of where the tech debt is. Classify easy fixes vs. fundamental architecture.

- Once you get traction, start fixing tech debt by allocating a part of engineering capacity for refactoring. Clean up a little on each release.

- Culturally, make it as cool to work on refactoring as it is build new stuff to sell. Set expectations that refactoring is part of every engineer's job. Recognize great refactoring. This is harder than it sounds.

Team debt manifests itself as a company grows and is also virtually unavoidable. Team debt manifests in two ways. First, when iterating rapidly toward PMF, the team will be small, and some members will wear many hats. Startups shift early team members from one role into another not because they are the "A-player" right person for the job, but they are "right person right now" that the startup has to keep things moving forward. Second, if the startup shifts directions away from the initial Founding Idea, a number of original team members become disaffected, are quietly (or not so quietly) still attached to the original idea.

Advice solutions for team debt

- *Replace or add leadership to address "right person right now" situations once the company starts to get traction. Hire a "background recruiter" to discretely scout A players to swap in.*

- *If some early employees aren't emotionally vested in the revised PMF mission, ask them to move on to a new mission and give them a graceful exit.*

Achieving PMF: A huge milestone

Finally, it all comes together. After countless iterations, endless customer meetings, long days and long nights, the enterprise startup achieves PMF. The startup has a hotspot customer problem with urgency, a working product, and paying reference customers who use the product and recommend it to others.

Finding PMF is a huge milestone on the enterprise-startup journey. Be proud. Celebrate!

Startup teams learn a lot as they iterate to PMF. They learn not just from customers that they won but also from those that they lost.

And not just from customers who moved fast but from also from those who moved slowly. These lessons don't just help them find PMF, these lessons are a critical input to the next stage of unlocking enterprise growth: Go-To-Market Fit.

Punchlines

» Enterprise PMF is different. Enterprise PMF requires paying customers who use the product, and recommend the startup's product to their peers.

» The path to PMF involves listening, experimenting, and iterating. And iterating not just on the product, but also on the target customer and the pain point.

» Over-focusing too early can be just as damaging as being too broad. Actual PMF may be adjacent to the initial idea. Finding the customer hotspots that lead to PMF often requires casting a slightly wider net around the initial idea, which can feel like heresy to passionate founders.

» The CEO, product team nor investors determine PMF. The customers and sales team decide.

» Finding PMF sometimes requires leaving early customers behind. This is okay, even if it feels terrible.

» Achieving PMF is a critical survival-phase milestone, and almost always comes with challenges such as tech debt and team debt.

» While PMF is incredibly important for an enterprise startup, PMF is not sufficient for unlocking growth. Get ready for the next phase: GTM Fit.

CHAPTER 3:
GO-TO-MARKET FIT

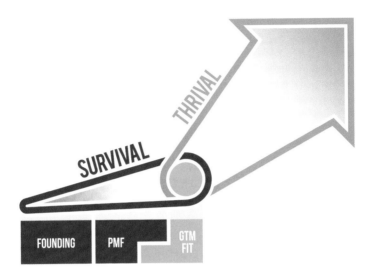

When many enterprise startups get to PMF, they feel they're ready to take off. "We have product-market fit! Let's go! Hire sales! Invest in marketing! Spend!"

The unfortunate frequent reality kicks in. Instead of sales taking off, sales just bump along. The number of new customers grows sporadically, painfully disproportionate to the rapid increase in sales and marketing.

"We hired sales and invested in marketing, and the only thing that went up was our cash-burn! We're frustrated. Our investors are antsy. What gives?"

What gives is this: PMF is sufficient to create growth and acceleration in consumer startups, but it's not sufficient to create growth and

acceleration in enterprise startups. The enterprise journey is different.

Many enterprise startups get to PMF but don't achieve growth and acceleration.

Why? Because there's a "missing link" between PMF and accelerated growth for the enterprise startup journey. Oddly, this missing link doesn't have a name or definition, let alone a structure or advice for how to deal with it. Until now.

The missing link for growth: Introducing Go-To-Market Fit

The missing link is something we call Go-To-Market fit, or GTM Fit. We think it's every bit as important for enterprise startups as PMF.

Developing and achieving GTM Fit is the number one thing about building a business that enterprise startups miss. Too often, founders and early investors assume that rapid growth will immediately follow PMF. This is natural. They believe strongly in the product and the market opportunity.

PMF does not factor in how a startup found and won its customers, how repeatable its wins are, and what those wins cost. But rapid growth for an enterprise startup only comes when the company can line up PMF with a go-to-market strategy that repeats and scales to go after customers. GTM Fit does all of that. It provides early proof of your GTM strategy and reveals early signs of momentum and growth.

So, what exactly is GTM Fit?

Bob: *"This may sound simplistic, but you have GTM Fit when you have a 'Yes' answer to these two questions: 'Do you feel customers pull you in? And, do you have a one-page playbook for repeatable wins?'"*

Finding GTM Fit is hard. The stakes are high. The search is stressful. It creates cultural and organizational changes. At the same time, it allows you to win customers, and that's energizing. Seeing patterns emerge that can be repeated makes everybody in the company realize that they're not crazy. Hiring grade-A talent becomes much easier. You pick up momentum, and it's a blast.

The 3 parts of GTM Fit: Model, Playbook, and Urgency

Let's break things down. Finding GTM Fit is a challenge that has three parts:

Go-To-Market Fit: 3 parts

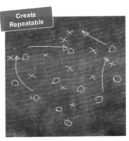

GTM Model

Direct, Channel, Web, Freemium, Trial & Upsell Marketing-led, Sales-led

GTM Playbook

Find & Win Customers What's <u>The Wow</u>? Align Everyone

Urgent Wave

Why buy <u>now</u>? Part of larger wave?

Figure 9 - 3 parts of Go-To-Market Fit

GTM Fit Part 1: Decide on a GTM model

Every startup has to decide how it will market and sell its product. That's what go-to-market means. GTM models abound: direct sales, inside sales, channel, freemium, web, land/expand, and more.

Early-stage startups cannot simultaneously support multiple GTM models. That's because it's impossible in the beginning to get repeatability when executing on more than one model. So startups have to decide on just one model that works.

But how? The answer depends on things like target customers, the customer decision-making process, the type of product, the price point, the gross margin, and onboarding time. Often the best approach is to experiment with early customer engagements to see which model seems to work best.

A good primer on picking a GTM model is *Leslie's Compass*. The author, Mark Leslie, was the founding CEO and chairman of Veritas Software.

Leslie's Compass: A Framework for Go-To-Market Strategy

https://www.linkedin.com/pulse/leslies-compass-framework-go-to-market-strategy-mark-leslie

At the highest level, all GTM models have to do four things:

1. Make customers *aware* of the product.
2. Get them to *evaluate* the product.
3. Close them to *purchase/commit* to the product.
4. Develop the right *pricing/packaging* to encourage commitment, purchase, and expansion.

GTM models range from heavy-touch (requiring significant human sales involvement) to moderate touch (partially automated, partially human) to light-touch with self service (no humans). Figure 10 illustrates a range of GTM models.

GTM Models

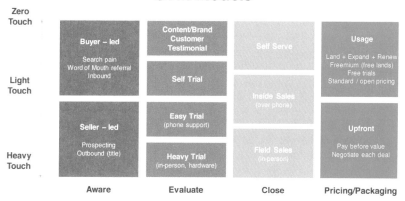

Figure 10: Components of GTM Model

Heavy Touch

The traditional enterprise-GTM model is heavy-touch and requires a person to lead most steps. While marketing generates leads (awareness), an experienced inside sales rep prospects for and qualifies potential customers (awareness), manages a trial (evaluation) and then signs a deal after multiple in-person meetings (closing/commitment) for a specific price (upfront payment). This model is effective but also expensive.

Light Touch

Companies pursuing a light-touch model replace much of the human-intensive work in each step with more automation across the GTM model.

- **Aware.** Digital marketing is replacing a lot of the lead generation and prospecting work previously done manually—and less efficiently—by expensive sales reps. With digital marketing, customers are attracted, engaged, nurtured, educated, and qualified—without the involvement of a person. Only once a customer is qualified does a sales rep get involved.

- **Evaluate.** Automated product evaluations enables customers to start using the product immediately. Automation requires an easy sign up and onboarding either as a cloud service or as an add-on to a platform that the end customer already has in place (such as Salesforce). The product itself becomes part of the sales evaluation process, rather than sales calls or slide presentations.

- **Close/Commit.** Usage during the evaluation stage drives customer value, justifying customer commitment. Usage data during the evaluation stage provides clues to sales reps for how best to help a customer commit.

- **Pricing/Packaging.** Light-touch pricing and packaging accelerates the value to customers while reducing (or deferring) the effort and cost to both customers and the startup. The goal is to provide immediate gratification and value for minimal initial pain and effort, and to fit within the user's budget. For example, the initial product might be free but have limits in time, usage or functionality that become clear over time to customers, who later upgrade to a paid version. Example companies include Cloudera, Slack, and Splunk.

Zero touch

Companies following a zero-touch self-serve sales models completely automate almost the entire awareness-evaluate-committ-pricing cycle. Self-serve is not for every product or customer. The user and economic buyer are typically the same person. Products must be easily understood, easily consumed, and easily supported. For example, a new class of companies are using the zero-touch model to sell products to software developers and developer operations teams. Marketing is tuned to speak to the developer, who is both the user and the buyer. Simple download, integration, and build tools combined with developer support are just as much a part of the product as the product itself. Self-serve can have very attractive unit economics: around 25 percent of revenues are spent on sales and marketing, versus 50 percent for average enterprise startups. Examples of companies using a successful self-serve model include Atlassian, Mailchimp, SendGrid, and Twilio.

GTM Model evolves over time

Picking a startup GTM model depends on the product, price point, channels, and most importantly the customer and the customer's buying motion. And, in some cases GTM models evolve over time, beginning as human-intensive to validate key assumptions and practices, and then later automate the GTM model with technology, product, and process.

GTM Fit Part 2: Create a repeatable GTM playbook

The core of GTM Fit: a playbook that allows a company repeatedly to find and win customers. A company that has this kind of repeatable playbook is on the path to acceleration. A company that doesn't have it risks bumping along in frustration and wiping out.

Nailing GTM Playbook 1.0 is critical to finding GTM Fit. Once in place, Playbook 1.0 becomes the blueprint for the marketing and selling motion of the company. It is also a powerful tool to ramp new sales reps and marketing people, and to align the rest of the company behind a go-to-market plan

But here's the catch: founders typically can't build Playbook 1.0. Founders know the product too well and their founder status changes the dynamics of a typical customer engagement. Instead, Playbook 1.0 comes from the real life experience of early sales reps and marketers.

> **Bob:** "During early sales calls we had a whiteboard outside one of the cubes that said 'What worked' on the right and 'What didn't work' on the left. We took notes on what kept a customer on the phone, what got to a second meeting, what caused a customer to invest time, and what caused them to move forward. And soon a funny thing happened: other parts of the company started paying attention to that list. It influenced our marketing slides. When we hired new salespeople, we used it as our starting point in teaching them. We didn't realize it, but those notes were our first draft of our GTM Playbook."

Playbook 1.0 has to be simple. If the playbook diagram doesn't fit on one to two pages, it's not ready. Getting there is harder than it sounds. It takes distillation, sacrifice, and constant iteration on the ground with sales and marketing reps.

Bob: *"I learned the magic of the GTM Playbook from MobileIron's early VP Sales, John Donnelly. The first thing John did when he joined MobileIron was to take our fledgling Playbook 0.5 and make it a real Playbook 1.0. I made the mistake of thinking this was just a sales-pitch thing. Boy, was I wrong. The playbook gathers and distills all sorts of things: value propositions, sales processes, customer engagement, and what everyone in the company needs to do to find and win customers. Playbook 1.0 became the core operating system for our go-to-market strategy and helped everybody in the company line up behind it. Nailing Playbook 1.0 played a key role in catalyzing the acceleration of our business in 2010."*

So how do you create a Playbook 1.0? Take the following steps, and then iterate, iterate, iterate.

GTM Playbook Step 1: Figure out the core stages in your GTM model.

Learn the steps that your early sales, marketing, and product team use to move potential customers through the customer journey. Write it all down. The GTM motion could be high-touch sales-led, light-touch marketing-led, or zero-touch self-serve.

Don't immediately default to the sales stages already programmed into the startup's sales system. Take a step back and think what the "real-world" steps should be that relate to the physics of the customers buying journey, not percent-likely-to-close forecasting buckets. The sales system can be adapted to the playbook, not the other way around. Figure 11 shows some examples.

Playbook Stage Example

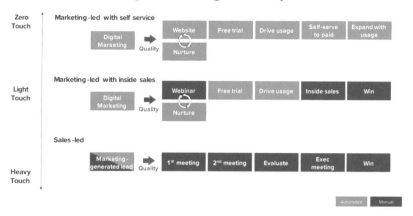

Figure 11: Define the stages of GTM Playbook - Heavy/Light/Zero Touch

GTM Playbook Step 2: What marketing and sales say and do?

What happens in each stage is the foundation of the repeatable sales playbook. Marketing knows what to do. Sales knows what to do. The playbook becomes a great teaching tool for onboarding new teams. But nailing all of the "say-and-do" stuff down is harder than it might seem. One company finished 50 percent of its playbook in three hours—but then took another three weeks to finish the remaining 50 percent! Distilling everything down to one or two pages forces focus and sacrifice. Distillation will uncover different leaders or parts of the organization have an 80-percent-similar view of the GTM motion, but 20-percent-different view. GTM assumptions that were implicitly understood across the marketing, sales, and product must now become explicit and 100 percent aligned.

GTM Fit: The huge cost of "only 20%" misalignment

The startup iterated on different aspects of GTM. The startup now has functional heads for sales, marketing, product, and customer success. The leaders are mostly on the same page for the GTM playbook, but they have a 20% different view. 20% different means 80% the same, right?

Unfortunately not. The 20% on which the four leaders differ is actually a different 20%. That means 0.8 same x 0.8 same x 0.8

same x 0.8 same = .41 same. That means that, to the rest of the company trying to execute the startup's GTM plan, the leadership team is only 41% aligned and nearly 60% misaligned on the GTM playbook, making it almost impossible to achieve GTM Fit.

Everyone will have an opinion about what matters most. And everyone will have to sacrifice ideas or historical habits they cherish. The biggest debates will happen here. This is hard work and requires quality time, typically dedicated multi-hour blocks every couple days for several weeks. It is some of the most important GTM work that a startup team will do.

What marketing/sales say and do

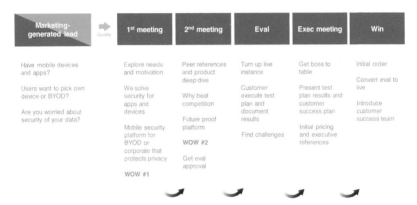

Figure 12: Example of "Say/Do" for Sales-led playbook

Find the "Wow!" Every product or service that's being sold has a "Wow!"—something in the pitch, the demo, the eval—that brings home the value proposition. A killer feature. A killer demo. A killer slide. A killer quote. Something that converts a moderate prospect into an energized opportunity, or from a trial customer into a champion for your product. When you find the Wow, you can see the body language change, interest level increase, or usage accelerate.

Frustratingly, the "Wow!" isn't usually found by asking the product team. It's found by watching and listening to customers during the marketing and sales process. And sometimes it's a secondary feature or capability.

When you find the Wow, amplify it in pitches, build it into evals, and in some cases make changes to the product user interface to highlight it. There can be "Wow!" moments across different stages of the playbook. Also, the "Wow!" changes over time, due to competition and changing customer needs.

GTM Playbook Example: Marketing-led for recurring businesses

Enterprise startups are increasingly pursuing marketing-led playbooks that leverage a combination of low-touch automation to find and nurture customer opportunities at the front end of the playbook and remote selling (known as "inside sales") at the back end of the playbook to secure customer purchases. This combination offers both lower cost of sales and easier to scale.

Marketing-Led Playbook
Recurring business

For products sold with a recurring business model, customer renewal is a critical part of the business model, which creates several important differences in a GTM playbook. In a recurring business model, the first signed contract is not the end of the playbook... it's just the beginning! Instead of "win" or "close", the customer is making a "commitment". The playbook becomes explicit about "live production" usage, the number one task to ensure successful renewal, and then "renewal" which becomes a large part of the GTM playbook in a recurring business.

GTM Playbook Example: Self-Service

In the case of a marketing-led playbook, more of the engagement is done through marketing and automated tools before a sales rep gets involved, whereas in sales-led playbooks, sales reps do the experimenting and iterating. The mindset for each, though, is the same: test, learn, discuss, iterate.

Figure 13: Example Self-service GTM playbook

GTM Playbook Step 3: Tools from company to support each stage

Under each stage of the playbook (highlighted in gold in the MobileIron example below), clearly identify the tools and deliverables needed to support that stage in the playbook and move customers to the next. Ask "What are the key things we need to nail this step in the playbook?" Typical deliverables include sales tools, marketing videos, digital marketing SEO/SEM campaigns, customer presentations, key "Wow!" product features, legal agreements, evaluation guides, onboarding guides, etc. The list depends on the playbook. The list of tools become top priority deliverables for the team and becomes part of the muscle of the sales motion.

Defining the list also has a very beneficial side effect for the rest of the company: the cacophony of seemingly endless requests from the GTM team to the rest of the company now makes sense. The playbook becomes a very powerful way to line up the different aspects of an early stage company behind the GTM strategy. The playbook provides clarity and motivation to the rest of the company—engineering, product managers, marketing managers, support managers, and others—to see how the thing they are working on ties into the overall go-to-market plan for the business.

Bonus: Playbook becomes foundation for sales metrics

The playbook becomes the basis to define your metrics and measure your business. By tracking volume inside each stage, movement between stages and dates, companies can (1) identify conversion metrics, pipeline number and dollar volume, sales cycle time, and (2) provide an early warning system to identify issues where prospects get stuck or drop out.

Figure 14: Stages provide basis for metrics

MobileIron: Completed sales-led playbook

The end-end playbook feels dense. Yet, condensing the entire GTM playbook—stages, reps say/do, and the tools to support each stage—onto a single page is a powerful exercise for the startup. (See following page)

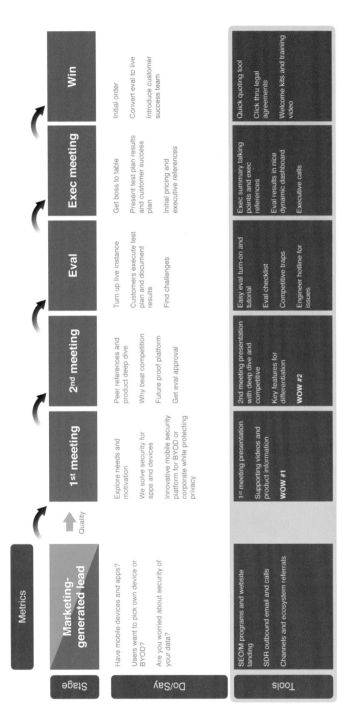

Figure 15: End-to-end example - Sales-led playbook [MobileIron]

Stage	Marketing-generated lead	1st meeting	2nd meeting	Eval	Exec meeting	Win
Metrics		Quality				
Do/Say	Have mobile devices and apps? Users want to pick own device or BYOD? Are you worried about security of your data?	Explore needs and motivation We solve security for apps and devices Innovative mobile security platform for BYOD or corporate while protecting privacy	Peer references and product deep dive Why beat competition Future proof platform Get eval approval	Turn up live instance Customers execute test plan and document results Find challenges	Get boss to table Present test plan results and customer success plan Initial pricing and executive references	Initial order Convert eval to live Introduce customer success team
Tools	SEO/M programs and website landing SDR outbound email and calls Channels and ecosystem referrals	1st meeting presentation Supporting videos and product information WOW #1	2nd meeting presentation with deep dive and competitive Key features for differentiation WOW #2	Easy eval turn-on and tutorial Eval checklist Competitive traps Engineer hotline for issues	Exec summary talking points and exec references Eval results in nice dynamic dashboard Executive calls	Quick quoting tool Click thru legal agreements Welcome kits and training video

MobileIron: Translating the sales-led GTM playbook to action

GTM Model — MobileIron followed a sales-led playbook where marketing generated leads and then handed off qualified leads to sales which then move them through the sales stages.

Marketing — lead with the 2-3 story hooks to grab customers interest. Tools focused to drive leads and qualify them. *Goal: convert leads to become 1st meetings.*

1st Meeting — introductory call or webinar with simple messaging and education. Tools included presentations, simple videos, and the first Wow (show separation of work and personal data on a BYOD device). *Goal: 2nd meeting for deep dive meeting with relevant parties.*

2nd meeting — deep dive meeting with business and technical stakeholder. Prove value proposition, share long term vision, and provide peer references. If necessary, drill into competitive differentiators. Tools are more technical, plus the 2nd Wow (the "Enterprise App Store"). *Goal: customer commitment to spend time on a product evaluation, which means customers get serious.*

Evaluation — Customer live evaluation of product to prove value proposition and competitive superiority. The hard part: mobile was new; customers often didn't know how to evaluate. Therefore, a critical tool was the evaluation check list and test plan to help the customer, and of course highlight advantages. Evaluation checklist was a living document regularly updated due to new capabilities or competitive tactics. *Goal: Ask for executive meeting to present results of test plan. The evaluation stage content was reversed engineered to maximize impact of executive meeting.*

Executive meeting — Present successful evaluation report, share long-term vision of company, and discuss execution capabilities to ensure successful product rollout. Tools include evaluation report, executive presentation, and personal calls from CEO or other company leader. *Goal: business approval to select MobileIron and buy.*

Win — Sign initial order and begin rollout and activation. Tools include quoting tool, legal agreements (preferably click-thru), and customer onboarding program. *Goal: successful rollout and happy customer who buys more.*

SendGrid: Sample for marketing-led playbook with self-serve

A successful marketing-led self-serve GTM strategy is difficult. Early on, the startup must market and create awareness and persuade customers to commit to the product. SendGrid, a cloud based email service, attributes much of its early success to its participation in the 2009 Techstars accelerator program and partnerships with startup accelerators, incubators, and others in the startup ecosystem.

To avoid the expensive ongoing customer acquisition costs typical of high-touch enterprise sales models, a self-serve product must provide a frictionless user experience and be immediately useable. In designing an easily accessible product, the startup then reduces the barriers that typically accompany the purchase of business software and can attract more customers to try, buy, and derive value from their product.

Sameer Dholakia, CEO of SendGrid, believes a self-serve GTM model requires the full commitment of the company—across marketing, sales, support, and, most importantly, product. The product must be designed to be bought without help from a salesperson. Even the culture of the company must be geared to self-serve. At SendGrid, it started with the founders wanting to build software to make the lives of developers better and easier, and that meant minimizing time spent with salespeople. Easy to say, but hard to do.

SendGrid's self-serve GTM required the complete alignment of four factors:

1. A well-understood problem: a specific value proposition (clear pain and use case) that is well understood by the market (without lots of education).

2. Clear PMF: product clearly solves the problem, and the problem matters.

3. A single buyer who is reachable: the user, the buyer, and the decider are the same person and one who can be targeted using digital marketing.

4. Fast time-to-value: product is easy to buy, implement, and get initial value from.

More advanced self-serve GTM models involve a product-led GTM model where the product itself is designed to guide customers to consume more and upgrade to higher value feature packages.

Nailing the GTM playbook.

Nailing Playbook 1.0 is critical to achieve GTM Fit and unlock enterprise growth. Iteration with customers, sales reps, and marketing is crucial to build the GTM playbook. Forcing distillation and alignment across the teams is painful but becomes the essence of repeatability.

GTM Playbook Summary

The results of a good playbook, whether sales-led or marketing-led, are the same.

1. Marketing/Sales **know what to do:** Defined and repeatable steps
2. Marketing/Sales **know what to say:** Key tasks and value prop points for each step
3. Rest of company **knows how to support each step** with tools, programs, and product capabilities that help the company win. Be sure to **find the "Wow!"**
4. Bonus: **Source of metrics that matter**

Once GTM Playbook 1.0 is nailed, the process to develop a GTM playbook is very repeatable and extensible. For most enterprise startups at any stage, crystalizing the GTM Playbook for new customers is the highest priority. Then, startups often create additional GTM playbooks for upselling customers, renewing customers, and even bringing new products to market. Building GTM Playbooks becomes a core differentiator and execution expertise for the startups that want to build a fearsome go-to-market machine.

GTM Fit Part 3: Line up on a wave with urgency

The first two parts of GTM Fit by themselves, picking a GTM model and developing a repeatable GTM Playbook 1.0, are not yet sufficient to unlock growth. Unfortunately, some startups achieve PMF, 20 paying customers, and have a repeatable playbook, but unfortunately line up on problem where customers don't have urgency to act now. As a result, sales cycles stretch out. Or, the problem is on a smaller tapering wave, generating a relatively small number of opportunities. To unlock growth and achieve GTM Fit, the playbook must be lined up on a customer problem that is both a sizeable wave (lots of opportunities) and has urgency (why now). If the GTM playbook is not lined up on a sizeable wave with urgency, growth will be a painful slog. When a GTM playbook is lined up on a sizeable wave with sufficient urgency, growth and acceleration happen.

Address an urgent operational pain

The urgent operational problem won't feel like a sexy way to transform markets, but it's important, because it creates the entry for the enterprise startup, and motivation for immediate customer action. Urgency answers the very simple question: Why buy now, not six months from now?

Provide a high-level strategic-value proposition tied to a larger wave

Enterprise customers buy now because they have an urgent problem to solve, but the key to earning a long-term customer is to ideally tie your pain-solver to a strategic value proposition that helps the customer achieve a longer term goal and is part of an increasingly important wave over time (e.g., digital transformation, cloud migration, mobile enterprise, consumerization of IT, etc.) For example: MobileIron's entry point pain was secure smartphone email, BYOD, and get apps, but the high-level strategic value was enable mobile as a first class citizen and enable user productivity.

There are huge benefits of surfing on an emerging large wave. The wave will generate urgency and awareness with potential customers and GTM partners—as well as investors, star employees, and potential acquirers.

Lining up for GTM Fit requires sacrifice

The startup achieved PMF, with customers clustered around the several hotspots. As a result, the GTM team now has a pipeline of potential customers clustered around those hotspots of pain points and buyers. Understandably, any deal that brings in revenue in a reasonable time attracts attention from the GTM team and absorbs GTM bandwidth.

GTM Fit requires making the tough choice to line up the GTM playbook and GTM resources on one or two customer problems with the most urgency, and then sacrifice the pursuit of legitimate customer opportunities that are tied to lower urgency problems outside the playbook. Sacrificing legitimate customer opportunities will drive a revenue-goaled GTM team crazy. The CEO and Board will feel pressure as well. But it's a necessary sacrifice. Focusing the GTM playbook on the right urgent problems is the final link in the chain for GTM Fit and growth!

When to start looking for GTM Fit?

Start looking for GTM Fit midway through the search for PMF. Why? The customer interactions at the latter part of PMF provide major clues for and help inform the iterations to find GTFit.

In particular, pay close attention to customer behaviors during the latter half of PM Fit: what got their attention; why do they spend time with you; who commits and who doesn't; who moves fast and slow; why did they buy and why did they not; and who actually makes the purchase decisions. The mixture of positive and negative data points are hugely valuable market signals for finding GTM Fit.

What if GTM Fit feels elusive?

Sometimes a company just falls into GTM Fit. Purchase orders are emailed in with minimal effort. The company can't follow up on most of the leads it gets, and deals are easy to close. But that's not common. Most companies struggle, iterating through trial and error to find GTM fit.

When GTM Fit eludes a company, one of two things is usually going on:

1. **Playbook problem** – Lack of repeatable playbook that nails one use case with enough urgency to drive leads and catalyze purchases *now*.

2. **People problem** – Different parts of the organization are not lined up on what's in the playbook, often due to past inertia or differing interpretations of the playbook

Cure #1: Find the GTM patterns

When the use case and problem don't create a sense of urgency, and instead just feel "nice to have," that's a problem. It needs to be fixed. Start with the customers you have won. What made them act or what cause them to get stalled? Is there a consistent profile for customers who found the use case urgent? Does that profile naturally exclude the lost deals and uninterested customers? If so, that's a clue to the ideal customer profile.

It's also possible that the problem is urgent but you haven't found the "Wow!": that key metric, feature, or report that captures the attention of buyers and drives them to buy your solution rather than the competition's. Get inside the head of the user and the buyer: What makes the buyer a hero? What are they scared of? What do they aspire to? What pain is solved?

How do you find the patterns? Identify the ideal customer profile? Find the pain? Tease out the "Wow!"? Your customers, prospects, sales and customer success teams will tell you. Every win, loss, stuck deal, or uninterested customer is the world teaching you. The key: move from anecdotes to analysis and visualization. It can be a very powerful exercise to bring together and look for patterns in the who, why, and why nots, and then make them visual.

Customer Visualization

	Happy Customers and won deals	Churned Customers and lost deals
Who is the buyer?		
Why now?		
Why win? Lose?		
Deal summary?		
How sell?		

Find the GTM Patterns

Ideal customer profile

Wow + Pain + Use case

Figure 16: Customer pattern visualization for GTM Fit

Cure #2: Get everyone in line

The other major challenge with GTM Fit is when different parts of the organization—typically sales, marketing, and product—are not lined up on a common GTM playbook, or aligned on 80% of the playbook and not aligned on 20% of the playbook. No one is being malicious or stupid. It's frighteningly normal. Here are some examples:

- **Misaligned Leads.** Marketing is using customer profiles, search terms, and messaging that drives lots of leads, which feels like a success, but those leads don't clearly have the pain or use case that requires the product. The leads don't fit the ideal customer profile.

- **Misaligned Deals.** Sales teams are given incentives to go after large upfront deals, yet the sales playbook and historical deals point to a small initial deal followed by expansion. Deal pursuit doesn't match the playbook.

- **Misaligned Product Focus.** The "Wow!" capability that motivates the customer to act is seen by the product team as unsexy and technologically uninteresting, and therefore doesn't get proper engineering attention and marketing awareness. The product team has not elevated the "Wow!"

- **Misaligned problem or use case across functional teams.** The most fundamental and common misalignment is that all teams are not pointed at and prioritizing the same problem or use case. This is particularly common as the startup adds new executive leaders for each of the different functions. Everyone is moving fast and has a slightly (or not so slightly) different conception of the problem or how different customers experience the problem. The answer: the CEO and the team executives must force themselves and the company to line up on the same early use cases and customer focus. Easy to say, hard to do.

To figure out where the team is stuck and misaligned, try constructing something like the table on the next page.

Align Organization to GTM Playbook

Learn from happy customers to drive sales, marketing and product

	Start	SALES (...can repeatedly close and win)	MARKETING (...find lots of good leads)	PRODUCT (...evaluate the wow and make users passionate)
	Happy customers			
Who has the problem	Title of active user? Title of decider?	Buyer champion/Primary user Exec approver/whose budget	Target customer profile Search/Messaging/Landing	Expand the ideal customer profile
Why act **NOW**?	Caused urgency to look? Drove rollout and usage? Favorite "hero" feature? Story? Key: Listen to customer talk about pain and tour solution	Clear pain and urgency Help buyer become hero Find the "Wow"	Illustrate pain/Use case Buyer aspiration or fear Content to show the "Wow"	Elevate the Wow in the product
How to sell	Customer metrics/justification for sale, expand, or renewal Peer references and Case studies	Buyer champion/Primary user Exec approver/whose budget	Help buyers learn Qualify, move along, nurture Content for each stage	Drive usage and value to make users into passionate advocates

Figure 17: Framework to align Sales/Marketing/Product on GTM Playbook

Above all, learn from the happy and successful customers who are using your product and understand its value. Also learn from customers who got stuck or said no. Both sets of customers are the flywheel that drive the development of Playbook 1.0, line up the leadership team behind the playbook, and create GTM Fit to unlock growth.

Finding GTM Fit: Hard on you. Hard on the team.

> **Bob:** *"The search for GTM Fit is at the same time—great fun, super frustrating, and very high pressure"*

Fun: Finding and winning first deals. Detecting signs of momentum. It's energizing!

Frustrating: Feeling so close—because you have PMF and some very passionate active customers—but you don't quite have the answer. Why aren't sales moving?

High Pressure: Cash burn ratcheted up from having a full engineering team to achieve PMF, and an early GTM team struggling to achieve GTM Fit. Yet, growth has not unlocked because the company has not achieved GTM Fit. The pressure is amplified given the timeline to find GTM Fit is never clear.

The stakes go way up during the search for GTM Fit. Everybody begins to feel the strain. Anxiety builds. Raising more money is hard, because even though you have PMF, growth has yet to materialize without GTM Fit. The natural founding enthusiasm starts to dissipate without hypergrowth as later deals seem just as hard as the early deals. The iterations of the GTM playbook feel like thrashing to the technical teams. If the search for GTM fit drags out, doubts creep in: the team and the board wonder about the viability of the business. Yet, everyone needs to stay motivated—from the office manager all the way to the board. The CEO must walk a fine line: convey optimism (GTM Fit is right over that hill!) while maintaining credibility.

Some who believe PMF is sufficient to unlock growth will recommend that the sample answer is "hire more sales" or "invest more in marketing"—essentially spend your way to GTM Fit. That rarely works. The pressure to hit the gas on sales and marketing will be enormous, but don't do it until you can see the repeatable GTM playbook and GTM Fit. Setting an explicit GTM Fit milestone with the board and the leadership team will help everybody manage expectations and create focus. Once you have GTM Fit and feel the momentum, *then* it's time to hit the gas!

GTM Fit: Strains the company and the team

- *Business strain:* Stakes and cash-burn go up. Very measurable goals are easy to hit or miss.
- *Culture strain:* Transition from product-led model to a balanced product-GTM model creates culture changes, particularly around how company makes decisions on GTM vs. product.
- *Execution strain:* Customers, sales, and marketing now demand X or Y in order to hit sales goals and achieve GTM goals. The product and engineering teams can't meet every new demand in the desired time.
- *Organization strain:* Execution threads must now be synchronized across sales, marketing, product, engineering, and support. Everybody feels stretched.
- *Market strain:* Competition rears its head. While you're searching for GTM Fit, others have started to go after the same opportunity.

VP Sales dilemma: Davy Crockett or Braveheart?

During the search for GTM Fit, one of the classic and most important questions: When to hire a VP Sales?

Conventional answer: When it's time to start selling. Our answer: We generally disagree, for two reasons: (1) No grade-A VP Sales will be the first sales person in the door, and (2) grade-A VP Sales don't author playbooks from scratch—they finish and scale them.

The better early path to GTM Fit is to hire Davy Crockett–style salespeople who can "find the path through the woods" by iterating and experimenting on sales to find and win early customers. The Davy Crockett-style sales rep develops early versions of the Playbook and gets the company close to GTM Fit.

Figure 18: Davy Crockett

Most grade-A VP Sales will intuitively recognize the difference between PMF and GTM Fit and choose to wait for clear signals that the startup is close to GTM Fit. What's the first thing a grade-A VP Sales candidate will want to do? Talk to early sales reps and early customers to see if there is a repeatable pattern that will scale!

Then, as the company gets closer to GTM Fit, it's the right time to hire the VP Sales. An exciting startup on the cusp of GTM Fit becomes a very attractive opportunity for grade-A VP Sales.

Once aboard, the newly hired VP Sales will polish the playbook, build and army, and then—like Mel Gibson in the movie Braveheart—lead the go-to-market army into battle against the enemy!

Figure 19: Mel Gibson playing William Wallace in the movie Braveheart

GTM Fit doesn't always mean hypergrowth now

Don't panic if the company isn't in hypergrowth mode. For some very good companies, growth kicks in later.

In some cases, a startup's GTM Fit simply will not have hypergrowth potential. This can happen if the customer base is small but growing, or customer buying decisions are lengthy. The startup may have to build on this lower but solid growth path. If so, manage fundraising expectations and be more deliberate about building the business with a cash-efficient business strategy. The good news is that lots of companies have moved from a slow growth path to a quicker growth path—if they can survive long enough feel the acceleration.

> *Tae Hea: "StrataCom had GTM Fit but was on a moderate growth path, going public after six years at a mere $100 million valuation. But then the market accelerated and significant growth kicked in. Cisco bought the company four years later for $4 billion."*

Inside the black box of GTM metrics

A good GTM playbook generates the framework for key GTM metrics and helps us measure and tune the the GTM business model.

Instrument the GTM machine analytics

Every GTM strategy can be viewed as a black box with one input (sales and marketing expenses) and one output (billings). Inside the box, between the input and output, is the GTM machine.

Figure 20 is a picture of the black box that shows the key elements of that machine:

GTM Black Box

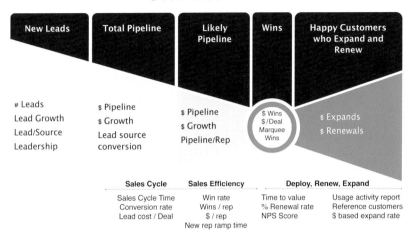

Figure 20: Unpacking the GTM "Black Box"

This illustration raises a core question: For every dollar put into sales and marketing in the front end, how many dollars of billings pop out in the back? Having a handle on each of these numbers, and the key efficiency ratios they represent, will allow you to do three things:

1. Measure where the go-to-market machine is getting better or getting worse.

2. Find a basis for sales forecasting and modeling.

3. Determine if you've achieved GTM Fit.

GTM metrics: Answer the key GTM financial questions

The GTM metrics helps answer the three fundamental GTM financial questions:

1. How *productive* is the GTM machine?: For every dollar in, what comes out? This is "GTM productivity," the ratio of incremental revenue generated for each additional $1 invested in GTM. If the GTM productivity is 1.0, then $1 invested in GTM generates $1 of incremental revenue.

2. How *predictable* is the GTM machine?: How do I model investment and forecast growth?

3. How *elastic* is the GTM machine?: How fast can I grow billings with additional investment, and where are the bottlenecks? Can the GTM playbook scale with incremental investment? Without GTM Fit (a scalable and repeatable GTM playbook), doubling the GTM investment will dramatically reduce GTM productivity, thereby generating minimal incremental new revenue while significantly increasing the cash-burn.

Answering these three fundamental GTM financial questions in the affirmative makes the company attractive to late-stage investors.

GTM Foundation: Unit Economics and Customer LTV

In addition to the GTM metrics, there is another category of metrics to pay particular close attention to: Unit Economics and Customer Life Time Value (LTV). Unit Economics of customers, over the lifetime of the customer (how long until they churn), delivers the Customer LTV.

Strong Unit Economics, combined with low churn, lead to strong Customer LTV. It is dangerous to scale GTM with poor unit economics around customer deal size, gross margin or customer life time—even with promising GTM metrics around customer acquisition or GTM efficiency, unless one truly believes that scale (lots of customers) will fix poor unit economics.

Figure 21: Unit Economics

Customer LTV is the ultimate root of value and reason to invest in sales, marketing, and product to build the business. Customer LTV metrics are critical to raising capital from late-stage or public markets. With strong Customer LTV, reasonable GTM metrics around customer acquisition and sales efficiency, plus a reasonable level of predictability, rational investors will see the return on investment and plow in growth capital at a reasonable price.

GTM Efficiency: What do you get out for what you put in?

Unit economics are driven by the product value proposition and cost structure. GTM Efficiency is driven by deal size, sales cycle, and overall how the startup's product is marketed and sold. GTM efficiency gets to the essence of how well a startup finds, wins, and keeps customers given particular resource investment. The measures of GTM Efficiency can be divided into three categories: Customer-acquisition-cost metrics, $-based efficiency metrics, and renewal-metrics.

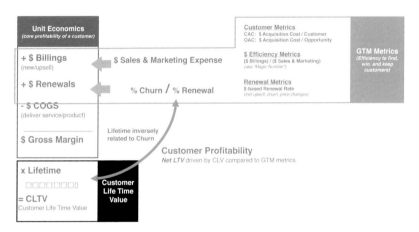

Figure 22: Bringing together Unit Economics, Customer LTV, and GTM Metrcis

Note that the lifetime of a customer on the left is inversely related to the % churn in GTM renewal metrics. The lower the churn %, the longer the customer lifetime.

Comparing Customer LTV with GTM metrics indicates the cost to acquire customers. The blue arrow above determines Net LTV which is the largest driver of overall customer and business profitability.

Metrics that signal GTM Fit

What clues in the metrics tell a startup that they have achieved GTM Fit?

The biggest signal: a noticeable increase in GTM efficiency, typically measured by generating more opportunity pipeline and closed deals with the same GTM resources. For sales-led and marketing-led GTM playbook, the signal is to see the increase in pipeline and converted deals across at least three sales reps. For pure self-service GTM playbooks, the signal is typically more than 10/deals per month. In either case, the key is that the increase must be seen across enough of the GTM team to signal repeatability, rather than a fluke driven by a single team or situation.

Be on the lookout for GTM leverage

Finding GTM Fit delivers repeatability through a playbook. That repeatability provides a linear ability to invest resources to drive sales results. This is great. During the search for GTM Fit, be on the look out for opportunities to create GTM leverage. What is GTM leverage? GTM leverage provides acceleration by providing larger returns on GTM investments, such as larger deals or faster sales cycles. It's like a bicycle shifting to a faster gear. For every turn of crank pedal, the wheel turns more times. Or even better, by creating non-linear returns on GTM investments, such as by attachment to another product, by a large channel that drives leads and deals. Finding sources of GTM leverage become a key lever during acceleration (see chapter 4: Accelerate to Category Leadership)

GTM leverage example: MobileIron

GTM Fit: MobileIron built a repeatable playbook with urgency around securing iPhones and enabling BYOD. That playbook drove early growth. The more sales and marketing investment, the more sales pipeline and deals.

Leverage Clue: MobileIron noticed that many larger companies, such as mobile operators and app vendors, wanted to increase their sales of phones, plans and apps to business customers. The need for security slowed down their sales. By adding MobileIron to their deals, their deals would get larger and go faster.

Creating GTM Leverage: MobileIron created lead genera-tion partnerships and channel reseller arrangements with mobile operators and mobile application vendors. The partners won because their deals accelerated. MobileIron saw a rapid increase in leads, sales pipeline, and deals thanks to the larger sales reach.

Leverage Results: rapid acceleration in top line revenue with only a modest increase in sales and marketing expenses, creating significant leverage in GTM metrics.

What does GTM Fit feel like? Momentum

Enough of the GTM Fit analytics. What does GTM Fit *feel* like? It feels like surfing with momentum. What does the lack of GTM Fit feel like? Paddling around in the water with no momentum. Signs of GTM Fit, or the lack of it, come from across the business. Here are some of the good and the bad.

GTM Fit   No GTM Fit

- Feel momentum and growth
- Leads grow organically
- Incremental investment in sales and marketing make leads and sales pipeline grow
- New reps quickly learn what to do and win
- Rest of the company knows what they need to do to support the GTM plan

- Post PMF sales bump along even after investment in sales and marketing
- Closing deals requires executive hero selling
- Every deal is different
- New reps struggle to learn

GTM Fit: Exit Survival mode.
Get ready for Thrival

Achieving GTM Fit is a *big* deal! The startup now has a product with multiple paying customers who refer their colleagues, as well as a repeatable sales and marketing playbook that finds and wins customers with a sense of urgency. The startup has earned the right to no longer be in Survival mode. The startup no longer needs to fear imminent death. With GTM Fit, it's time to shift gears to into Thrival mode, drive growth and GTM Acceleration. Very few companies ever make it this far. Getting here is a huge accomplishment. Stop and enjoy the moment!

Punchlines

»   PMF is not enough to unlock enterprise growth. There is a "missing link" between PMF and enterprise growth.

»   The missing link is GTM Fit. Without GTM Fit, companies can bump along on a low-growth path. GTM Fit is:

1.   A clear GTM model

2.   A repeatable GTM playbook

3.   Lining up on the right use case to create urgent demand.

»   Finding GTM Fit is hard and requires iteration, just like PMF. During the search for GTM Fit, stress levels and cash-burn go up. Cultural changes and execution challenges are normal.

»   A classic mistake in the search for GTM Fit is to hire the VP Sales too early. Instead, hire the Davey Crockett salespeople to help find the company's GTM "path through the woods".

»   Achieving GTM Fit and defining GTM playbook 1.0 is a major milestone. GTM Fit means that a startup can invest in sales and marketing to drive rapid growth.

»   During GTM Fit, instrumenting the GTM machine for the proper metrics to address sales productivity, predictability, and elasticity enables the startup to make decisions about growth and attract a new class of investors.

» Towards the end of GTM Fit, be on the lookout for opportunities to create GTM leverage, which will help drive acceleration in the next stage.

» Achieving GTM Fit means the end of Survival mode. The company now transitions to Thrival.

CHAPTER 4:
ACCELERATE TO CATEGORY LEADERSHIP

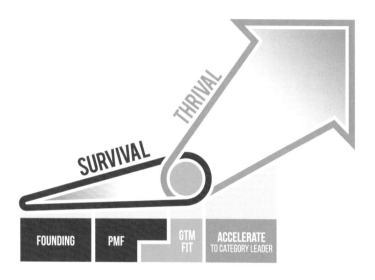

FOUNDING | PMF | GTM FIT | ACCELERATE TO CATEGORY LEADER

Welcome to Thrival

The startup had its "Thrival moment"—the moment when you shift from trying not to die to figuring out how to win. This is a profound event in the life of an enterprise startup. CEO's vividly remember their "Thrival moment" when the game changes.

Thrival moment: Rocking chairs at a leadership offsite

Tien Tzuo, CEO & Co-founder, Zuora

"Zuora was founded in 2008 to provide a business platform that would underlie and enable the subscription economy. In our first few years, our customers were primarily other startups, but by 2011, we started to win customers across different industries and geographies.

I remember our Thrival moment vividly. It was the summer of 2011. We were sitting in rocking chairs on a hotel patio after our Zuora leadership offsite. Earlier that day, our sales-engineering team leader, Matt, put up a slide that showed the logos of the customer prospects in our sales pipeline. We all looked at the logos. All were Fortune 500. Some international. It was a great list. Then Matt said, 'Either we win them, or our competition does.' I remember thinking, *What? This isn't a wish list, these were active deals. Companies with active projects. And an amazing list of companies.*

It was a wakeup call. Our business had gradually shifted from 'evangelize' to 'find and win.' That evening, after an intense rocking chair discussion on the patio, I said, 'The game is different now,' and we all looked at each other and nodded. From that moment on, we shifted from survival to Thrival."

Thrival moment: "Holy crap! Every vertical has the same problem"

Aaron Levie, CEO & Co-founder, Box

"Founded in 2005, by early 2009, Box had about $5M in revenue with a large base of individual users, and it was seeing early enterprise customer traction. Early enterprise customers were spread across different verticals— healthcare, consumer goods, and professional services. According to the classic 'bowling pin' or 'crossing the chasm' analysis, we hadn't yet found the repeatable pattern. But we dug deeper. We went customer by customer, and dug into the specific problems each customer used Box to solve. And this led to an 'Aha!' moment: every customer, regardless of vertical market, used us to solve the same problem. I remember thinking, *Holy crap! Every customer— regardless of vertical—has the same problem. We found a horizontal problem that has urgency. It's just a matter of time. We can target the common problem and repeat rapidly across verticals.* We had our repeatable playbook. We had found our Thrival moment."

Thrival moment: VP Sales making a big bet

Bob Tinker, CEO & Co-founder, MobileIron

"In the summer of 2010, MobileIron had been winning early customers. We found a problem with urgency—securing iPhone and enabling bring-your-own-device (BYOD). We started to see repeatability.

The 'Aha!' moment for me was late summer 2010. Our VP Sales, John, came into my office and said, 'I see customer opportunities in the pipeline. My team can't get to them all. I'm willing to raise quotas and take on a bigger number if we can hit the gas on hiring.' John saw the wave of opportunities and had the repeatable playbook to go after them. He needed the people. When our VP Sales was willing to put his neck on the line with that kind of confidence, we knew we had found our Thrival moment. We hit the gas and never looked back."

Accelerate GTM to category leadership

After GTM Fit, it's time to accelerate and spend. Even if that feels reckless. You've earned a chance to win, and you have to make the most of it. Goals now become simple: Accelerate the business, become the category leader, and stay out in front.

Making the shift from Survival to Thrival and accelerating to category leadership is a blast. The shift also requires major changes in execution and mindset. Rapid growth and acceleration strain execution. They're messy and change how everyone works. Decisions have to be made differently now. Everybody will be stretched to their limits.

You've got major momentum and are accelerating quickly. This leads to big questions. How fast can the startup go? When to hit the brakes? When to turn the wheel? How to maintain control while accelerating? The stakes are higher now than ever before. Make a mistake at this speed, and you'll crash. Do things right: build tremendous value and achieve the goal you had at the outset of this journey—become the category leader.

Why target category leadership?

When a startup achieves GTM Fit and starts to accelerate, it usually isn't alone. Competitors are accelerating too. Together, everybody is creating and defining a new category—and the race to lead it is on.

It pays—a lot—to win that race. A study published in the *Harvard Business Review* ("Why It Pays to Be a Category Creator," Eddie Yoon and Linda Dekeen, March 2013) made this very clear. "To find out just how lucrative category creation can be," the authors write, "our company examined *Fortune's* lists of the 100 fastest-growing U.S. companies from 2009 to 2011. We found that the 13 companies that were instrumental in creating their categories accounted for 53% of incremental revenue growth and 74% of incremental market capitalization growth over those three years."

Becoming the fast-growing category leader creates a virtuous cycle of customers, investment, and talent that drives growth and reinforces leadership, as shown on the right.

Market categories are somewhat fluid. Let's skip the formal definitions of markets and categories, and focus on the practical implications. A market category must be *distinct*, *viable*, and *large enough* to be tracked and competed separately. Market categories bring order to chaos, especially for customers. Market categories help customers segment business problems and vendors into logical

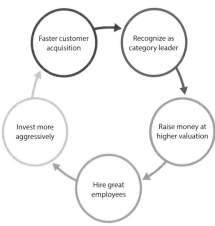

Figure 23: Virtuous Cycle of Category Leadership

groups, and then evaluate which vendors in those groups best solve the customers' problems.

Vendors don't decide. Customers and industry analysts do.

Startup vendors don't decide category leadership. Industry analysts publish research reports distinguishing leaders, however, evaluation criteria is imprecise. More importantly, top customers heavily influence category leaders by sharing product decisions with industry analysts and other customers. Facts and data also play a big role in shaping leadership, as does market noise and PR.

> **Bob:** *"After winning our early customers, we worked our tails off to win our first few lighthouse accounts, the ones we know would make other customers say, 'Wow, you have so-and-so!' Our first was a large bio-tech company. Then a large pharma company. Then a large European bank. They referred us to their peers. Then more and more. The thought-leading customers influenced each other and the industry analysts—and helped us emerge as a category leader."*

Category leadership helps create a shortlist of vendors for customers to consider. It generates leads. It creates credibility. It influences potential hires and investors. It helps accelerate the business.

Advice for creating a new category

Many startups create a new market category. The good news: creating a category automatically gives you a jump on becoming the category leader. The bad news: creating a category is hard. Every startup tells the market that it is creating a new category, but few customers believe it. Very few startups *actually* manage to do it.

Define the category early

Defining an emerging category is an art. The category has to be significantly different from existing categories. It has to be big enough to address enough problem points for customers while being small enough for the startup to be a leader. And every emerging category needs a name—something catchy and differentiated from existing categories that can become a hot trending search term. This, too, is hard. In most cases, competitors will be trying to define and name the category differently. Pay close attention and try to influence this process.

Focused competitors add legitimacy

Embrace the competition. Being alone will not convince the market that a category is emerging. Category creators need competition. What tells the market that a new category is emerging? A healthy number of competitors, all focused 100 percent on the same problem.

Reinforce with respected customers

Every industry has thought-leading customers whom everyone in the industry watches. When a thought-leading customer identifies a distinct problem and then buys a particular product from a focused company, the market sees a new category being created.

Validate by media, analysts, and experts

As the market for the emerging category picks up enough momentum, premium media (Wall Street Journal, TechCrunch) will start to recognize and name the emerging category. Influential industry experts use blogs and social media to define an emerging category. Analysts (Forrester, G2Crowd, Gartner, IDC, etc.) will demonstrate their thought leadership by characterizing the new emerging category.

GTM Acceleration drives massive changes across a company

GTM Acceleration toward category leadership drives substantial shifts across a company—in execution, mindset, market, and investors. We've organized some of the most-important shifts in the table below.

Execution	Mindset
Careful execution → Calculated recklessness	Survive → Thrive
Careful executives → Executives who ramp	Product-led culture → GTM-led culture
Conserve cash → Spend to win	Iterate → Speed wins; fix as you go
Focused wins → Aggressive land-grab	Stingy hiring → Fast hiring

Market	Investors
Work in obscurity → Obsess about awareness	Early-product investors → Growth investors
Market development → Thought leadership	Find PMF-Fit → Growth and unit economics
Few competitors → Separate from the pack	Prove can sell → Plausible path to profitability

Execution shift: From careful execution to calculated recklessness

Survival requires frugality and cautious decisions. Once a startup has momentum from GTM Fit, it's time to drive growth and cement category leadership. This requires calculated recklessness and aggressive risk-taking. The early executive team, who so carefully conserved cash through the survival phase, now needs to ramp aggressively. The sales and marketing leadership rapidly turns the crank on the GTM playbook, aggressively establishing clear category leadership before the competition. The product team rapidly invests in new product capabilities. The company accelerates, focusing on growth and increased market share. This feels reckless, but it's *calculated* recklessness: choosing to take reasonable gambles to go fast and fix later. You're building a pipeline of talent larger than the hiring plan, rapidly expanding while simultaneously shoring up foundations and putting basic processes in place. Some leaders can make the shift from careful execution to calculated recklessness. Others cannot.

Market shift: Separate from the pack

Build a massive pipeline of target customers. Win lighthouse customers that other customers follow and respect. Secure major channels that provide access to customers and reinforce your market leadership. At the same time, expect the competition to intensify. The market has noticed your product. With GTM Fit, startup competitors will see the acceleration and mimic your moves. This is normal. You wouldn't want to throw a party and have nobody come!

In time, adjacent, larger incumbent players will shift gears to also enter your category, confusing customer prospects. Sales efficiency can drop as hand-to-hand combat in seller-led customer deals intensifies. As incumbents begin to copy messaging, marketing yields in marketing-led selling can drop. This is also totally normal.

There's magic when you figure out how to break through the increased competition, separate from the pack, and accelerate into position of category leadership. We've already talked about the first two ways to generate this magic: (1) Win on product-market fit, and (2) out-execute on the right GTM playbook. But there's something else to do now: (3) Use thought leadership to win.

Market shift: Obsess about awareness and thought leadership

Be obsessed with awareness. Any mention of your industry should mention you. Woo industry analysts: Are they listing you as a category leader? Have you influenced them to create a new category? Are they amplifying your problem to potential customers?

Be obsessed with thought leadership. It enables smaller companies to own mindshare inside customers' brains, influence customers, and influence the market. It is where smaller, more nimble, more advanced companies can have an advantage.

Thought leadership drives both brand awareness and category leadership

A category emerges when customers have become aware of a problem, are learning about it, and are seeking a path to success. Everyone is looking for advice and clear information from a thought leader. A passionate founder providing a mix of vision and practical advice can quickly become a thought leader in an emerging category.

Knowledgeable early-startup team members become the go-to-source of information for customers and industry experts, which also organically reinforces awareness and brand. For example, Jon Miller, cofounder of Engagio and previously a co-founder of Marketo, invested heavily and early in thought leadership by writing the definitive book in the account-based marketing category, blogging frequently, and speaking at events. Engagio, by creating original and valuable content in the new category, has the number-one organic (non-paid) search position. Thought leadership by an enterprise startup drives awareness and perception of category leadership.

Thought leadership: Earn customers' respect

When founders become thought leaders, they educate the market and customers, and make themselves known as valuable members of the community who are out to help the industry. Ray Carroll, the VP Sales at Engagio and a former VP Sales at Marketo, describes thought leadership this way:

> "[It] gets you into the buyer's subconscious without having to sell. Thought leadership is the ultimate 'give to get.' Since you've given free (and mostly neutral) advice on how to help the buyer, the buyer will look at you differently during the sales process."

Thought leadership: Elevate the customer conversation beyond features

Often a customer will begin a meeting with an enterprise startup founder by presenting the founder with a list of priority one requirements derived from existing products and vendors. This sets up a legacy player to win. A savvy founder doesn't play that game. Instead, a savvy founder elevates the customer conversation by attacking with thought leadership and making the customer see that there's more than just comparing features. It's about catalyzing change, being part of "the new way," embracing new strategies, solving emerging technology challenges. In this new conversation, the legacy player quickly becomes viewed as obsolete, and the startup now sets the agenda.

Thought leadership: Be authentic. Be provocative.

To be effective, thought leaders have to provide advice tailored to the emerging category and deliver it in a distinctive, authentic voice. Most importantly, that advice has to be valuable to the customers. Provocative thought leadership can help drive awareness by creating controversy, but it can also risk alienating the majority of customers still attached to "the old way." It's a tricky balance. But startups have a great advantage over incumbents: they can deliver provocative thought leadership at a time when incumbents are delivering muddled messages to protect legacy positions.

Marketo: Thought leadership helps customers succeed personally

Marketo's thought-leadership strategy began with a simple message: Marketers deserve a seat at the revenue table alongside the CEO and VP Sales. The company said, "Join the Revenue Revolution and help build the Marketing Nation." Through blogs, books, definitive guides, and its events and meet-ups, Marketo established itself as a major resource for marketing professionals who wanted to get ahead. For example, a young marketer flew across the country at her own expense to attend a Marketo conference. Why? The event offered her a chance to learn from and network with the best marketers in the business. And she wasn't alone: more than 5000 people attended the event. Becoming a Marketo expert helped launch the career of many marketers.

Mindset shift: A GTM-led culture

With GTM Acceleration, a company shifts from a purely product-led culture to a culture that balances product and GTM-led, which can create huge cultural tension.

- **Priority tension.** Company priorities are now influenced by sales and customers, not product and technology. The product teams often get frustrated ("We're losing the soul of what got us here—our product").

- **Resource tension.** Rapidly growing headcount on GTM team feels imbalanced to the existing engineering and customer-support teams, who are getting pummeled by the speed of the growth ("We're barely holding it together back here, and we keep hiring more outbound people!")

- **Compensation tension.** Sales reps and leaders who beat sales targets can earn big paychecks, which annoys everybody else ("Why do they get paid so much? Everyone contributed on that deal!")

Be ready for this. Take solace in that this happens in most companies.

Nine times out of ten (there are notable exceptions), the difference between a good company and a successful company (presuming both have a solid product), is a fearsome GTM machine. That's what can drive company growth to new levels and, ultimately, category leadership. All equity holders in an enterprise startup win when the GTM machine wins.

Mindset shift: Speed wins. Fix as you go

When a company hits GTM Acceleration, speed matters. The time for careful iteration is over. It's time to go—and to go fast. Win customers. Open up channels. Build customer support. If there's an issue, try to fix it, and circle back later to address it. Perfect execution is not the goal.

This shift creates huge tension between, on one side, those who make up the growth machine, who are pushing the company forward as fast as possible, and on the other side, the operationally centric parts of the team, who keep the wheels on the wagon. It's a *really* tricky balance: the company has to accelerate, go fast, and build up operational and product debt, but it also has to be sensible enough to fix what needs to be fixed to keep it together.

Mindset shift: Fast hiring

In the Survival phase, stingy hiring was the right model. Now in Thrival, having enough people to drive growth and build out the product becomes critical bottleneck to category leadership. Not having enough people can knock you off the leadership path. Recruiting, hiring, and onboarding becomes a core mission for the company, a core competency for every manager, and a key evaluation metric for each executive.

In GTM Acceleration, a company needs to build a recruiting machine. This is similar to building a sales machine. It requires a recruiting leader. It requires a strong "why you want to work here" story. And it requires a team of recruiters executing on a process with deep support from the hiring managers. To build a recruiting machine properly, create metrics to measure both pipeline and hiring by function, much in the way that pipeline tracking is done for sales. Good recruiters are good company sellers, and that's no coincidence. Recruiting and sales are very similar processes.

Aggressive hiring is hard. Instead of hiring 20 people a quarter during the survival phase, during acceleration you can easily hire 20 people a month—or week. It's a fundamental shift. Leaders can no longer hire from their past talent pools. Recruiting goes from an ad hoc, manager-led activity to a global core competency. Rapid hiring is *really* hard on hiring managers, who are desperately trying to execute and recruit at the same time. Keep an eye out for red flags:

- "I'm too busy, I didn't get chance to hire."
- "Green-light every candidate."
- "No candidate is good enough."
- "Recruiting isn't giving me enough leads."

Team leaders are no longer judged purely on execution. For leaders during GTM Acceleration, the ability to hire and build a team is equally important. Leaders for this stage now need to attract talent, make hiring a part of team culture, and hit hiring targets.

How to maintain culture during rapid hiring

Run a new-hire boot camp. Oracle is famous for this. There is *no excuse* for not having a new-hire boot camp. It's the prime moment for teaching new employees about the culture, the business, and the company goals, and for creating a network across peers in other teams. It's a pain, and it takes time, but you just have to do it. And it can't be just an "HR thing." It needs to be owned by an executive and have high participation from the leadership of the company.

Interview for culture fit. This seems basic, but it's usually poorly done. Train hiring managers to interview for not just technical or domain skills but also mindset and culture fit.

How to avoid "Bozo Creep" during rapid hiring

The problem is inevitable. As team leaders aggressively go after hiring targets, they become less thorough and less selective, and they hire some B players. Under so much pressure to deliver, they also become loath to let low performers go. Anyone who tells you this can be avoided hasn't been through aggressive hiring ramps. It's going to happen. So, what's the antidote?

During the hiring process:

- Insist on cross-team interviews outside of the hiring manager's direct team.
- Require "backdoor/blind" references (references the candidates do not give you themselves) before hiring someone.

After the hire:

- Focus on continually improving the quality of your teams. Set expectation that each leader should be replacing lower performers regularly. This is harder than it sounds.
- Give managers an "automatic swap out," in which they can replace a position if they let someone go for performance.
- Be gracious and respectful when letting someone go. A hiring mistake is on the company. How exits are treated is seen by the market.

Investor shift: Growth-centric

Survival stage investors are product- and team-centric. Thrival stage investors are not. They're interested in growth, momentum, and a plausible path to profitability. In particular, they ask three core questions:

- **Growth.** How fast are you growing? Can you keep it up? How big is the market?
- **Competition.** Why are you beating the competition? Is your position defensible?
- **Economics.** Does your playbook have decent unit economics? Is there a plausible path to profitability? What about cash flow break-even?

Growth investors care deeply about your operating plan and performance against that plan. Somewhat like public-market investors, they think in terms of "beat and raise": (a) Are you beating revenue targets? and (b) are you consistently raising your goals for growth?

Growth investors hyper-focus on valuation. How does the valuation at which they invest compare to the possible expected valuation in the public-market or late-stage acquisition? Growth investors can provide substantial capital at high valuations and bridge to the public markets. Growth investors can't help on product or early GTM strategy. But they can help when it comes to finding later-stage executives who have been through GTM Acceleration. Given their experience, they can also help early-stage CEOs anticipate change through acceleration and beyond.

The big question: How fast to go?

This is the most important—and hardest—question to answer. And you have to ask it again and again as you execute on GTM Acceleration. The answer depends on three factors and their related questions:

GTM Metrics & Sales Capacity

Cost/Opportunity and Cost/Customer vs. Life Time Value(LTV): What is the full sales-and-marketing cost for each new sales opportunity (Opportunity Acquisition Cost)? What is the full sales-and-marketing cost for each new customer won (Customer Acquisition Cost)? What is the Customer Life Time Value (Customer LTV) of each customer? OAC and CAC relate growth to sales and marketing investment. High LTV to CAC ratio increases company value with each customer won.

GTM Efficiency: What is the dollar value of new business won for each dollar of sales-and-marketing expense? What is the dollar value of total billings for each dollar of both sales-and-marketing expense? This represents a ratio of GTM efficiency on dollars in and dollars out. GTM efficiency goes down right after acceleration, but then stabilizes as acceleration slows. If a company is too efficient on this metric, it may not be investing fast enough. If it is not efficient enough, then slow down.

Sales Capacity: What is the quarterly quota capacity for a sales team relative to the business plan? If you add a new sales team, how fast does it ramp to full productivity? Sales capacity and ramp rates have a huge impact on cash-burn when accelerating.

Market Landscape	**Wave:** Bounded or Unbounded? Are you part of an explosive market wave that creates demand, limited only by your ability to spend? Or is it a market that will produce customers organically at a more-measured rate?
	Competitive Landscape: Is there an aggressive competitor or incumbent who looks poised already to grab category leadership?
Cash	**Cash Reserve:** Do you have enough capital, or can you raise enough reasonably quickly, so that you will always have a six month reserve?
	Financial Markets: What's happening in the public markets for your category?

Sample growth algorithms

As you consider the how-fast question, it's key to define the algorithm to use when deciding how fast to grow.

- **Pipeline algorithm:** Spend rapidly in lead generation and qualification. Then add a new sales team based upon pipeline thresholds. For example, for each additional $2M in pipeline created, hire a new sales team and assign quota. Repeat.

- **GTM-efficiency algorithm:** Use the "magic ratio" of New Annual Recurring Revenue divided by Sales-and-Marketing Expense to guide sales and marketing investment. Set ratio targets (depending on recurring or non-recurring businesses) where to invest more or invest less.

- **Land grab, only constrained by cash:** In an unbounded market-opportunity and supportive financial landscape, make marketing-and-sales efficiency assumptions, then build an operating plan that grows as fast as possible, only limited by the cash that you have. If you raise more cash, ratchet up plan. *Important note: In this model, early-warning indicators are critical. Miss a target, and cash-burn can catastrophically explode. Or the financial landscape can change, putting the company in jeopardy.*

GTM Acceleration increases growth—and risk. To drive an enterprise startup in GTM Acceleration, you need dashboards and early-warning systems that indicate when growth isn't materializing or expenses are out of line, in order to adapt *very rapidly*.

Like a racecar driver, in GTM Acceleration you are going full speed on a track full of competitors out to beat you. Your eyes are on the road ahead, and your dashboard tells you what's going on. Come up with a dashboard that displays the most-critical measures for your racecar. Typically, these are current quarter sales, expense forecast, cash burn, and cash balance—plus a forward looking combination of sales forecast and pipeline that serves as an early warning system.

Figure 24: Acceleration dashboard showing future sales, current sales, expense, and cash

Watch them all religiously. If things change for the better, you can go faster. If things change for the worse, react very, very quickly. React too slowly, and the company quickly will run out of cash and hit the proverbial wall.

Metrics are critically important, but nothing replaces the need for good field intelligence. The sales, marketing, and customer success teams will often have the best real-world view of what's happening on the ground in terms of leads, customer deals, competition and customer churn. Plus, they are the ones who will execute on growth. Listen to them. Calibrate the intelligence from the troops as yet another early warning system.

Chaos of GTM Acceleration: Really fun and really scary

As you move into GTM Acceleration and hit the gas, the speed becomes thrilling. You win customer after customer, leaving the competition in the rearview mirror. Top-line sales accelerate. Great people want to join the team. Investors are competing to help you grow faster and build a category leader (and are temporarily less concerned about profits). There are other kinds of thrills in startups, but accelerating is one of the most fun. Go as fast as you can. Optimize for speed.

At the same time, racing at speed will create strain and cause the business to wobble. Customer demands will increase. Product usage will ramp. Hiring and onboarding rapidly will become a challenge. Competition will intensify. Execution will get harder. As your car is accelerating around the track, parts of it will vibrate and wobble. It doesn't matter how skilled a driver you are: at this speed, if you hit a bump or miss a critical engine signal, you can crash.

No matter how well you plan and prioritize, things are going to go wrong during GTM Acceleration. You might grow your organization too quickly and fumble on execution. You might take on too much technical debt, causing customer satisfaction to drop. You might blow a major release for a customer and lose a big deal. A big company might buy a competitor, freezing customer deals. You might miss a quarter right as you're getting ready to raise another round of capital. You might ratchet up your valuation too quickly and eliminate room for mistakes.

GTM Acceleration raises the stakes. With GTM Acceleration, a company has a chance to be the category leader and matter. At the same time, more capital—and more careers—are on the line.

Fix one thing, another breaks: The flywheel of success and pain

Category leadership requires continuous acceleration. Every success milestone is an opportunity to celebrate. And, ironically, ever success milestone unlocks a new opportunity for pain. Welcome to the flywheel of success and pain!

Figure 25: Flywheel of Success & Pain

Sales growth: Predictability and pain

The sales machine has driven growth. Every quarter is a big top-line number and a big investment in sales and marketing. Forecast accuracy becomes more complex—and more crucial to the financial plan and investors. Everyone—the team, investors, and the market—has become accustomed to beating the operating plan. What happens the first time there is a missed forecast? Pain. Lots of pain. The forecast miss damages the confidence of your team and your investors. And to amplify the pain, a forecast miss typically triggers a rapid adjustment in spending and people.

Customer growth: Priority tradeoff between new and existing

Rapidly growing customers by the hundreds or thousands creates an avalanche of customer-driven product requests and support issues. New product capabilities are now adopted across an ever-larger number of customers. Technical glitches now impact more customers, and often more severely. The number of variables and use cases explodes as the product "interacts with reality." This creates a painful resource allocation choice between better serving existing customers and acquiring new ones.

> **Bob:** *"The rapid customer growth really beats up product and support teams. Six months earlier, engineering/product was iterating on PMF with a small number of customers. Now the same product is now being activated inside 100 new customers per quarter, with many large clients deploying it in mission-critical situations. The product and support team is simultaneously onboarding new customers, responding to an avalanche of support issues, and building repeatable processes. You can never have enough resources to get to everything. Someone is always feeling let down."*

Capital: Balancing temptation and reality

GTM Acceleration requires cash, and investors, logically, want to invest to fund the growth. The enthusiasm creates a temptation to ratchet up the operating plan targets in order to raise more capital and increase valuation. The operating plan gets wound so tightly that there is little room for error. Companies are tempted to get ahead of themselves on valuation. This feels great and minimizes dilution at the time, but any execution error raises questions about the valuation and creates the risk of a flat or down-valuation for the next round, which creates unnecessary damage to the psyche of a startup. Better to moderate valuation expectations, provide room for error, and create a reasonable progression of valuation.

Team: Straining to ramp

Rapid hiring and company growth is critical to achieve GTM Acceleration. But they also make maintaining culture and avoiding bozo creep more difficult.

Execs: Straining to change

GTM Acceleration changes the company. The CEO's role changes. Executives' roles change. Some teams are now larger than the entire company was just a short while ago. The question becomes: Which leaders can change to fit their new roles, or which leaders needs to be changed? (This question is a major theme for *Survival to Thrival Book 2 – The People Journey*)

Execution: Growth drives operational complexity

Acceleration rapidly increases operational complexity across the company. Dozens of new initiatives run simultaneously, straining the operational tracking capacity. Delivering on projects and initiatives requires increased coordination across teams. Forecasting future sales relies on an increasingly complex combination of marketing, sales, product delivery, and customer success. Success metrics change and become more complex, making it more difficult for the leaders and the teams to see what's really going on "inside the machine."

Product expansion: Platform plan or pain?

GTM Acceleration often includes some sort of platform expansion into adjacent product areas or markets. The core question becomes: Is this expansion part of a broader platform strategy or a distraction? Platform expansion requires major new development work, new product launches, new ecosystem development, and it increases overall complexity. If the engineering team objects, the GTM team says just hire more engineers, especially since the cost of capital is low during GTM Acceleration. Measuring the impact of new platform initiatives is challenging when compared to the mainline business investments. At the same time, iterations that took place during the PMF stage now seem like shortcuts that are coming home to roost as customer scale up. Tough tradeoffs are necessary between hardening existing products and expanding new platform capabilities to drive top-line revenue.

Becoming strategic to your customers:
A double-edged sword

The success: your product is strategic to your customers. The product matters to their business and operations. Customers create endless development requests for new feature modules, higher scale, and even new product lines. The pain: customers' dependency on your product injects a level of caution and rigor that seems to slow you down.

The flywheel is normal: Expect it and learn from it

Riding the flywheel is both exhilarating (the speed!) and painful (the problems!). Each time a new milestone is reached, a new set of problems comes into view. How everybody anticipates and addresses these problems makes the difference between flash growth, which quickly fades, and sustained growth, which makes category leadership possible. Acceleration creates a mixture of success and pain that is hard on the team and hard on the CEO.

> **Bob:** *"Acceleration is nuts. Lots of things break. The hard part: prioritizing what to fix, and deciding that the rest will just have to wait. It's a very painful thing to do, and it particularly sucks for the people whose problems don't get fixed. The message to them goes something like this: 'What you are working on is important. Keep working hard, but the cavalry isn't coming right now.' It sounds disingenuous, but it's the reality."*

The good news is that if your startup is on the flywheel, the business is accelerating toward category leadership. Every rotation of the flywheel is an opportunity to celebrate a success, and conquer a new challenging pain. This is totally normal. And represents a spectacular professional and personal growth opportunity for the company and the team.

The "Oh, shit" moments

Bad things will happen, guaranteed. Some will be self-inflicted. Some will be market-inflicted. Be mentally prepared.

> **Bob:** *"During the go-go times, when it seemed we could do no wrong, some of my team encouraged me to proactively remind the team that we will hit turbulence. I wish I had better heeded their advice. Expect turbulence. Prepare for it. How a team reacts to turbulence largely determines long-term success."*

When bad things happen, face it head on. Admit it. Come up with an action plan—and react quickly. Reacting might mean holding a key product release, cutting back on hiring, or cutting expenses. Reacting quickly to major issues is critical. During GTM Acceleration, quick reaction can mean the difference between life and death.

Losing the first big customer	There are few moments more vivid than the first time being fired by a big customer. Sometimes it's because of a deliberate choice that ended up failing to meet the customer's needs. Sometimes the team tries their best and the customer still fires you. It stings.
Losing a key executive at exactly the worst moment	The company is in the midst of a tough quarter or a difficult product release. Everyone is cranking and straining together to build the company. Then a key executive walks in to your office and says, "I'm moving on." Your reaction: "Now?! Seriously?" The cascading impact of the departure quickly flashes through your mind. What does this mean for execution? What does this mean for the team? What is the collateral impact? How are you going to explain it? This stinks.
Missing a sales target in the middle of capital raise	Top-line results matter every quarter. And they matter doubly when raising a round of capital. Missing sales targets in the middle of raising capital is messy. Best case: the miss only affects credibility and impacts valuation. Worst case: the miss scares off investors, and the capital raise falls apart, leaving the company in the lurch.

Deal with it head-on. Don't surprise investors after a financing close with a revised plan. The silver lining: the actions taken represent an opportunity to demonstrate understanding of the business to investors and your tenacity in the face of adversity, which can cement the credibility of the leadership team. |

With every "Oh, shit" moment, the key is to react calmly, objectively, and move through it. In most instances, the team will look to the CEO for implicit or explicit pointers on how to react. Each "Oh, shit" moment tests the leader's credibility, which in turn influences how effectively that leader can navigate the next test that comes up.

The upside: in some cases, the "Oh, shit" moments create a useful catalyst for change. A catalyst to drive changes more quickly than would happen when everything is going well. Takeaway advice: Never let a good crisis go to waste.

How to avoid total chaos

Clear vision and culture

During rapid growth, thousands of big and little decisions get made all the time. How does a rapidly growing team stay pointed in the same direction? Make difficult tradeoffs up and down the company? Integrate new team members?

The answer: By aligning on vision and culture. Vision keeps everyone looking in the same direction. Culture binds the team together in good times and bad, and provides guidance on tough decisions. (See book two, chapter four on Vision/Culture.)

Set explicit company and team goals.
Tackle interlocks and issues.

Top-level company and team goals	A CEO must set and communicate top-level company goals. These can be multi-year high-level goals, or the top goals for the next 12 months.
	Functional VPs need to have functional top-level goals for their teams. Best practice: (1) Make each leader's goals transparent and available to everyone in the company, and (2) Go over goals in new-hire boot camp.
Quarterly goals and regular leadership offsites	Get the leadership team together every quarter to track progress on quarterly goals and roll forward goals for next quarters. Identify and resolve issues. And just spend time together to strengthen the connective tissue between the exec team.
	When things get really busy during acceleration, often the team will resist—"We're really busy, we don't have time for an offsite this quarter." Do it anyway. Be religious about it. There is no substitute for quality time together.

Lots of companies use Google's OKR (Objective-and-Key-Results) model. However, for running a company and executive team, the OKR model is missing two major concepts:

1. Interlocks/Dependencies. One executive's goals often depend on another executive's execution. Make this interlock explicit by calling it out when you set goals.

2. Company-level issues. Often issues are tracked separately from goals. Raise company-level issues up to same level of attention and stature as company goals and objectives.

Pace of execution: Regular communication and program reviews

Regular communication sounds boring: Exec team staff meetings. Program and initiative reviews. Scrum sessions. Sales and marketing planning sessions. All-hands meetings. Meetings, meetings, meetings. It's obviously critical to watch out for and minimize stupid meetings, but execution requires regular structured communications and quality person-to-person or team discussion. Take the opportunity to re-engineer how communications and program reviews are done.

GTM Acceleration: Go fast, communicate, execute

Tien Tzuo, CEO Zuora

When Zuora entered GTM Acceleration and began to grow fast, Tien recognized the need to rewire communications so that he and his team could execute at speed. He implemented three key changes:

- Extension of the weekly exec-team meetings from one hour per week to three hours every week, with a once-a-month full day meeting.

- Commitment to offsite meetings of one or two days every quarter attended by an extended staff list of the top 30 managers, for planning and bonding.

- Changing of the operating model from hub-spoke with CEO at the center, to exec team as a "hive mind," where everything was brought to the exec team. As part of that change, Tien controversially killed one-on-one meetings with the CEO: problems were now brought to the executive team.

At each stage, adding another meeting or program review feels like the last thing anyone wants to do. Do it anyway. That's what leaders do. Execution depends on teams sitting down regularly to talk, brainstorm on a whiteboard, and coordinate execution. Execution depends on regular forums and business reviews to measure progress, uncover issues, and make decisions. Simply sending an email doesn't count as execution. Own the interaction. Drive the execution. Company success depends on it.

Accelerating to category leadership is both fun and scary

Moving into Thrival mode and accelerating toward category leadership is crazy intense. The stakes are high. It's uncomfortable. It's exhilarating. Your mission is simple: race to build a category leading business that delivers real value and makes a difference in the world. So accelerate, drive execution, be ready for the inevitable speed bumps, and hold on tight!

Punchlines:

» Welcome to Thrival! The company shifts to GTM Acceleration and calculated recklessness.

» The core goal of GTM Acceleration is to become the category leader. The trick is deciding how fast to go. When to speed up, when to slow down, and when to turn.

» GTM Acceleration requires a *profound* change in mindset, execution, and culture. Become a hiring machine. Obsess about market and thought leadership. Build your GTM Acceleration dashboard. React fast to issues. Speedy reaction is the difference between adjustment and hitting the wall.

» GTM Acceleration is hard on the team and hard on you. Things that used to work no longer do. You're on the flywheel of success and pain. Ironically, success brings the next set of problems.

» Bad things will happen, guaranteed. Some will be self-inflicted. Some will be market-inflicted. Be mentally prepared.

» Vision and culture, combined with a rigorous execution cadence, are the antidote for total chaos.

» The startup will exit GTM Acceleration a different company.

CHAPTER 5:
ACHIEVING SUSTAINABLE INDUSTRY LEADERSHIP

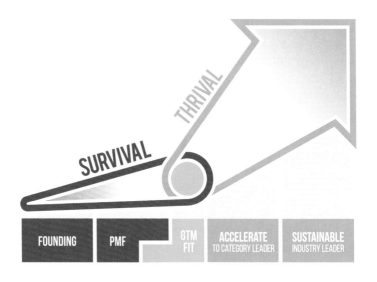

It's a long road for an enterprise startup to make it this far. The early team iterated their way to PMF and won early customers, taking some shortcuts along the way. They figured out GTM Fit with a clear GTM model with a repeatable playbook focused on an urgent problem. They then shifted to calculated recklessness, accelerating rapidly past a field of legitimate startup competitors out for blood. Big companies bought their way into the market through acquisitions. In all this time, every brain cell and muscle fiber in the company was focused on customer acquisition and engineering features to win and drive growth, often incurring technical debt and business debt. Through intense execution, team changes, painful speed bumps, and a healthy dose of good luck, the team accomplished the amazing: they created a real company with real revenue that is now a category leader. A spectacular accomplishment!

Now, the next challenge: to transcend from a fast-growing category leader to become a *Sustainable Industry Leader*. Fast growth category leaders on the path to sustainable industry leadership are typically newly public companies, raising lots of capital to fuel growth and tackle adjacent products and markets in order to become an industry leader. Sustainable industry leadership is yet another big challenge, but creates massive shareholder value and truly manifests the mission of the company. Some notable examples of companies that successfully transcended from category leader to industry leader include:

- Cisco transcended the router category to lead the networking industry.
- ServiceNow transcended the IT helpdesk category to lead the IT-operations industry.
- Splunk transcended the IT-analytics category to lead IT-machine data industry.
- Palo Alto Networks transcended the firewall category to lead network security.
- Oracle transcended the database category to become a leader in the enterprise-app industry.
- SAP transcended the ERP category to also become a leader in the enterprise-app industry.
- Salesforce is in the process of transcending the Cloud CRM category to lead the enterprise Cloud apps industry.

Enterprise startups who went public as part of the class of 2013 (Box, FireEye, Nimble, RingCentral, Tableau, Veeva), the class of 2014 (Aerohive, Arista, HortonWorks, Hubspot, MobileIron, NewRelic, Zendesk) and the class of 2015 (Atlassian, Pure Storage) and many others are in the midst of making the transition.

Challenge: Sustainability and transcending

The hard part: becoming a Sustainable Industry Leader requires that a company shift gears to become a sustainable (profitable) business *while simultaneously* transcending its initial category to become an overall industry leader.

Drive to Sustainability: Getting to the Sustainability stage requires both an execution shift and a mindset shift. Business goal shifts from "Grow, grow, grow" to "Grow sustainably." The execution mindset shifts from "Go now, spend now, optimize later" to "Make disciplined tradeoffs against our plan." Predictability and a path to positive cash flow become critical for new class of investors. Culture shifts to also value operational excellence and efficiency, creating conflict with the existing acceleration-centric culture. And, unsurprisingly, executive roles change again.

Transcend initial category to become an industry leader: Moving beyond the initial category to lead an industry typically requires a mix of three things: extend into adjacent categories through internal development or acquisition; expand its initial product to become multi-product platform and ecosystem; and add GTM models to reach into new markets. All of this generates turbulence and create a need for the company to re-find GTM Fit for the new businesses. Perhaps most challenging is that the company must undergo a mindset shift and refashion its self-image and its external image in order not get stuck in its initial category.

These two goals can feel contradictory. While driving to Sustainability, the company is simultaneously expanding scope of product and go-to-market to become an industry leader, which painfully accelerates the cash burn rate and re-introduces turbulence. Business tradeoffs get harder with the constraints and importance of predictability, driven by a new class of investors. Major competitors nip at your heels, hoping to capitalize on the startups more disciplined slower growth.

The shift is significant. At this point the company may have thousands of employees with major operations around the world where the culture and operations of the company are historically geared to growth. Now, the company must shift to more disciplined growth, while cleaning up and operationalizing the short cuts of fast growth.

The opportunity to become a Sustainable Industry Leader is an enormous opportunity create value and manifest the mission of what was a little startup struggling to survive. That startup is now a Thrival-mode category leader on the cusp of becoming a Sustainable Industry Leader. It's operating in rare air indeed.

Transcending the initial category

Unfortunately, not.

Mark Templeton, Citrix CEO 2001 to 2015, described his company's path to transcending its category. Citrix had achieved category leadership in the remote-access market with revenue of $527M and was very profitable. But the company was bumping up against the glass ceiling of scale. It had one product, one route to market, and a single focus on remote access. Everyone inside and outside of the company knew it needed an "Act II," a bigger vision that provides market headroom to grow. The goal became to double revenue to $1B top-line revenue—in three years. Executing on that $1B goal created another round of change, and turbulence at scale, in order to get to the next stage.

Project X-1: From $500M category leader to $1B industry leader

Mark Templeton, CEO Citrix 2000 – 2015

In order for us to become a $1B industry leader, we had to make a step-change as a company. We needed a bigger vision. Go-to-market changes. Product-conception changes. Team changes. We questioned many sacred-cow beliefs, organizations, and programs. And, the self-inflicted turbulence began.

Re-conceptualize our identity

We re-conceptualized ourselves and painted an expanded industry leading vision that took us beyond our existing category. We laid out this vision as a set of 10 ideas we called "Virtual Workplace," and even created a related YouTube video and printed booklet.

Figure 26: Citrix re-conceptualizing their identity

Plan to get there: Project X-1

In 2003, we laid out a multi-year plan for growth and change, and launched it to everyone—employees, investors, and customers. We called it "Project X-1," which was inspired by Chuck Yeager's journey to breaking the sound barrier. It was very important for everyone to understand exactly what the goal was, and their contribution to Project X-1. We broke the X-1 set of goals into smaller pieces for various teams to know their line-of-sight accountability to the mission.

- Core products needed to grow from $500M to $600M. We needed $200M from things we had neither invented nor acquired yet.

- Services teams needed to drive to from 3 percent to 9 percent of revenue mix.

- Every team needed a plan to double in size and reimagine their structure, workflow, and spans of control.

- We needed to start marketing like a $1B software company, instead of the one-hit software wonder that we were at the time.

Re-introduce turbulence

For Citrix, we drew this picture to help ourselves grasp what we were collectively embarking upon.

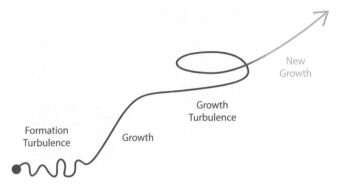

Turbulence is part of the flight to $1B

Formation
Turbulence

Growth

Growth
Turbulence

New
Growth

Figure 27: Citrix and self-inflicted turbulence on the way to $1B

It was also important to set team expectations about the impact of external forces and mistakes we would make. Project X-1 required a lot of faith in ourselves, and our ability to drive new products and routes to customers, neither of which we had ever done successfully. I guess it was more about persistence than faith. It was definitely a "burn the boats that brought us" time in the company's history. There were days when I had severe doubt in our ability to absorb all the needed change. Our employee population was on track to double. "Old-timers" were quickly becoming the minority. At one all-hands meeting, an old-timer asked, "Your growth message is great for newbies, but what's your message for old-timers?" My answer: "You gotta believe. You gotta believe in our plan, our team, and our vision. If you don't, you gotta leave to make room for believers." The room of 700 exploded with cheering. That moment was a seminal moment in the journey. By the way, many old-timers left, which was good for them and for Citrix.

The result

We hit $1B three years later. In fact, we exceeded the goal, reporting $1.126B! I remember the moment vividly. We had the scar tissue to show for it, but we would eventually move through $2B and $3B. We are proud of what we accomplished. And we never looked back.

Few companies transcend their initial category

Only 11 percent of the software and internet-services companies that reach $100M in revenue (roughly the size of a category leader) end up going on to reach $1B.

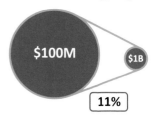

Figure 28: Only a small number of $100M revenue companies make it to $1B

These numbers come from a McKinsey study published in 2014 ("Grow fast or die," by Eric Kutcher, James Manyika, Olivia Nottebohm, and Kara Sprague). The study surveyed around 3000 companies active in the internet, application, gaming, and systems sectors between 1980 and 2012, and it established that between $100M and $1B, many companies run up against either natural market size or market share limits to their core product or service. To grow successfully to $1B and cement industry leadership, companies have to somehow transcend those limits.

The Seven keys to transcendence

McKinsey identified five common threads (paraphrased below) across those companies that successfully transcended to become industry leaders. To that list, we've added an additional two of our own.

Seven keys to transcendence

1. Expand from initial market niche to a broader horizontal, or to multiple verticals.

2. Deepen $-per-customer through expansion selling or the upselling of adjacent solutions (through internal development or acquisition).

3. Augment initial GTM sales approach by adding multiple sales models (and GTM playbooks).

4. Increase the bench strength of leadership (usually by building a new team).

5. Successfully bridge customers through a major product generation change, new standards, or technology change (sometimes called "re-platforming").

—Our two additions—

6. Create platform gravity around your products where customers and an ecosystem build capabilities that depend on your platform.

7. And most importantly, a mindset shift: reconceiving the self-image and external image of company to not get stuck in the initial category.

Each of the enterprise companies mentioned in the chapter introduction that successfully became a sustainable industry leader (Cisco, ServiceNow, Splunk, Palo Alto Networks, Oracle, SAP, Salesforce) executed on a mixture of the above strategies.

The path to industry leadership

The path requires a mindset shift and execution shift. Companies must reconceive themselves internally. And refashion their external image to avoid getting stuck in their initial category. Expand the vision to include the adjacent categories. Educate employees and the market about that expansion. Set company-wide goals specific to market adjacencies. Be willing to make targeted bets in the financial plan. Deliberately hive off energy and focus to overcome the inertia of core category market demands that would otherwise absorb all budget and energy. Succeeding in adjacent categories repeats the same process as in the core category: Find PM-Fit, find GTM Fit, and then accelerate to category leadership (although M&A can accelerate the process). In many ways, these new initiatives become the startup within the startup.

Execution Shift	Mindset Shift
Add new go-to-market Capture adjacent category Product → Platform & ecosystem	Category leader → Industry leader Overcome gravitational pull of initial category
Market Shift	Investor Shift
Industry competition intensifies New startups now gunning for you Catch-22: Avoid innovator dilemma	Public equity as an M&A tool to enter adjacencies

Add new GTM

There are lots of ways to add go-to-markets: adding a new customer segment (large enterprise, mid-market, small business), a new geography, a new channel, or a new sales model. In any of these cases, two things are key: (1) Developing and iterating on additional GTM playbooks for the new go-to-market (industry leaders can handle more than one playbook); and (2) devising separate metrics for results and resource investments to track progress, identify problems, and guide future plans.

Capture adjacent categories

Going to market with a new product isn't easy, regardless of whether it has been developed internally or acquired. The company may now have thousands of customers and a proven GTM team, but this does *not* mean that simply adding a product to the company's price list mean instant success. Far from it. Externally, the company has to educate customers and market experts, so that they no longer pigeonhole the company in its original category. Internally, the new product team needs to repeat the PMF and GTM Fit cycles for the new products to get early traction and build a new playbook. Existing product and GTM functions must overcome well-developed muscle memory to adapt to the new products. Habits and inertia create subtle bias inside the company towards the original core market, creating headwinds for the new products. Often the CEO must mandate company-level goals and back them up with specific incentives for the adjacencies to become a core part of the business.

A platform has two core characteristics: (1) Moving from selling one product to multiple products, and (2) an external ecosystem whose business depends on your platform. Expanding from a product to a platform with an ecosystem drives growth, deepens customer value, strengthens competitive differentiation, and supports long-term customer retention. Making the transition to platform often require retooling of GTM motion.

> **Bob:** *"At MobileIron, shifting from a single-product sales motion to a multi-product platform required everyone in sales, marketing, and our channels to change their sales playbook. This was a critical opportunity for us. Simply rolling out new sales training wouldn't work. We took a more drastic approach. Every single sales rep and field engineer had to present the new platform story directly to me or one of the other executives and answer product, pricing, and ecosystem questions as if I was a customer. That meant over 75 individual presentations for me alone. It seemed inefficient, but it was very effective. Ninety days later, the entire company's GTM motion snapped to platform selling, which drove our growth and cemented our leadership position."*

Ecosystem development clearly creates value for the startup, but the critical factor for a successful ecosystem is to create value for developers, partners, and customers that improves their business. The key is WIIFT—"What's in it for them?" Think of building an ecosystem the same way a startup would build a customer base—by clearly articulating a value proposition that convinces ecosystem partners to join your platform mission.

Competitive landscape: Eat or be eaten

Expanding into adjacencies and go-to-markets will mean a new crop of competitors. Large incumbent platform companies with deep pockets and market influence will now see a startup as a legitimate threat and will come gunning. Expanding focus to include adjacencies opens you up to your own innovator's dilemma—smaller, focused startups will now try to disrupt you in your core market with a fresh approach. Expansion from category leader to industry leader by definition means you are eating someone else's market opportunity. Others will try to do the same to you. In larger categories, billions of dollars are at stake. Expect companies to fight back. Expect others to come after your opportunity. It's how the market works. Be prepared.

Overcome the gravitational pull of the initial category

The time and energy that everybody in the company has devoted to the initial category creates powerful inertia. Self-identity as the leader in the existing category crowds out employees' ability to mentally engage in a new category. Ruthless focus on a single product and problem in the early days becomes company dogma. Financial plans, operational models, and even language and culture are all geared to the initial category. The GTM team expresses reluctance to create new playbooks to accommodate new categories. The product/engineering team deprioritizes changes to the core product that are required for the new category. The unpredictability of adjacent investments or M&A is tough on the financial plan and the board, who is at this stage of the company optimizing for predictable growth.

External industry analysts exacerbate the bias, pigeonholing the company in its original category. The inside team and outside customers pay attention to analyst-reported differences between category leaders rather than tackling adjacent categories that rapidly expand the company's opportunity.

"The category isn't your company"

Aaron Levie, CEO and Founder, Box

"Box was founded on enabling a new file-sharing model. During a 10-year period, we overcame hurdles and executed our way to category leadership in the Enterprise File Sync & Sharing (EFSS) category and going public on NYSE in 2015. Incredible accomplishment for the Box team!

While our mission and vision was always larger, our pride in becoming category leader in EFSS began to define us. We obsessed over analyst reports identifying small differences between us and other category leaders. Internally we prioritized resources based upon our category leadership. We sometimes let our initial category success constrain our self-identity.

That has changed. While we appreciate our category leadership position in EFSS, we work hard to not let it define us. Our vision and opportunity at Box is beyond EFSS—our opportunity is to unleash the power of collaboration at work across the cloud, mobile, and the desktop, fundamentally improving how people get their jobs done."

Achieving escape velocity

Overcoming the gravitational pull of the initial category is hard. It requires energy and focus. But it is very doable. Companies manage it differently, but here are some common approaches:

1. Paint the bigger vision and re-conceptualize company identity inside and outside. Educate and reiterate constantly. Assume this will take two to three times longer than you think.

2. Hive off teams and make focused financial investments outside the core historical category. Consider big moves, such as acquiring a company, as a catalyst for this shift.

3. Define company-wide goals and metrics that reinforce new adjacencies and expansions. Celebrate and reinforce major milestones along the way.

4. Be prepared for turbulence as the company creates new muscle memory that conflicts with old muscle memory. Ask those who don't adjust to the broader plan to move on.

Transcending the category is a spectacular learning experience for the leadership team, an exciting mission for the entire company, and an opportunity to create enormous value.

Big Question: When to shift from Acceleration to Sustainability?

Timing matters enormously. Shift from Acceleration to Sustainability too early and risk losing momentum as major competitors pass you by, missing the opportunity to move from category leader to industry leader. Shift too late and the extended Acceleration phase burns significant capital before proving the path to Sustainability, making late-stage and public investors wary. Without sufficient capital, growth slows quickly, projects tied to establishing category leadership are canceled, and the startup loses its market position. Time the shift correctly—and win big. Time the shift incorrectly—and fade.

How to know when it is time to shift to from Acceleration to Sustainability? Several signs that indicate it may be time to shift to Sustainability:

1) Execution breaks and jeopardizes the overall business

The rapid acceleration outpaced the company's ability to keep up, operational execution craters, customers begin to leave, early technical debt and business debt come home to roost. Even though the market demand is there, the company will need to slow growth, address execution, and pay down the organizational and technical debts.

Facebook made this transition in [May 2014]. Whereas Facebook's motto during the GTM Acceleration phase was "Move fast and break things," the company changed the motto to "Move fast with stable infrastructure," in recognition of the need for a more balanced approach. Outages related to execution damaged customers, the platform ecosystem, the company reputation, and the predictability for investors. The new execution model: speed coupled with discipline.

Facebook CEO, Mark Zuckerberg, takes the stage
at the company's F8 conference, April 2014

2) The physics of growth become harder

Here the "law of large numbers" applies. Growing by 50 percent a
year on $250M/year (adding $125M) is a lot harder than growing
by 50 percent on $100M (adding more than $50M). At some point,
as it scales, the company's machinery strains and loses efficiency.
Absolute dollar growth is often still large, but the percentage growth
is lower, which knocks the company out of the "high growth" group.
(Note: Rarely, a business can have such compelling expand/upsell/
renewal momentum that overcomes the law of large numbers. If
you have this momentum, don't shift yet!)

3) Supply of growth capital is thinning

Calculated recklessness (or GTM Acceleration) typically implies accelerated cash-burn, which defers "cash flow break-even" and requires significant capital funding. Growth-capital markets fund this "reckless" growth because they believe the long-term value of accelerated spending will later start generating huge positive cash flow. But the capital markets only fund it up to a certain point—specifically, when the next round of capital (public markets or otherwise) decide it's time to see proof and progress on the path to positive cash flow and profitability. And that "point" can suddenly change. Investors' appetites (or lack of appetite) for funding reckless growth depends drastically on market conditions. The decision to shift gears must be made *before* it's obvious. By the time it's obvious, it's too late.

4) Land grab vs. expand and upsell

The wild land-grab customer acquisition days are tapering. You and your competition have captured the customer base. Now you see a better lifetime value (LTV) for customers by expanding your footprint or adding new products inside existing customers rather than trying to add incremental new customers. Sales now shifts focus to more deeply penetrate existing customers. Customers also pull you into adjacent categories that make strategic sense for a platform extension. This has a useful secondary effect: because you are leveraging existing customer relationships, sales growth is highly efficient, generating disproportionate results for relatively modest capital and operational investment.

Drive to Sustainability

GTM Acceleration with calculated recklessness drives a company's mindset and execution. Shifting gears in order to drive to the Sustainability stage requires fundamentally changing that mindset and execution, which is particularly hard because those behaviors were, in many ways, the keys to success during GTM Acceleration. Changes happen across the board for the company:

Execution Shift		Mindset Shift	
Calculated recklessness → Predictable growth		Clear path to cash flow break-even	
Spend to grow → Sales efficiency/LTV		Any growth is good → Prune based on LTV	
Do now, fix later → Plan, metrics, operations		Culture and goals now a blend of growth and optimization	
Market Shift		Investor Shift	
[intentionally blank]		Predictable growth and path to profitability	
		Capital from public markets	

Execution shift: Calculated recklessness to predictable growth

Predictability matters. Blowing a sales forecast creates millions of dollars of swings in your cash balance, dashes late-stage investor confidence, and impacts market perception. Missing a product's ship date destroys big deals, risks your quarterly plan, and snaps morale. Internal and external predictability must become part of the sustainable company DNA.

The first test of predictability: *Is the business inherently becoming more predictable?* Expanding/renewing existing customers, rather than relying on mostly new wins, is inherently more predictable. A large sales force and well developed channels provide increased pipeline coverage on quarterly sales targets, which also becomes inherently more predictable. Inherent predictability matters.

Executing on inherent predictability, when possible, requires two things: (1) a real plan, and (2) operational tools to know if you're on or off target. Plans and operational tools cut across sales, product, marketing, and every team in the company.

Every decision of reasonable size that changes the financial plan must manifest in the plan with clear revenue goals and expense goals. Good metrics are also key: they'll provide an early-warning system that will reveal if previous assumptions and decisions were off track. This also creates good discipline. Different products or market segments that are at different stages of development begin to be broken out into different P&L plans, in order to provide more granular planning, decision, and measurement. This often runs counter to a historically functional-centric planning-and-tradeoff model, and requires an additional level of sophistication from the executive leadership team and the planning and finance functions.

There are two particularly high-leverage spots in the company that play a critical role in predictability:

1. **FP&A (Financial Planning & Analysis):** Everything from top to bottom in the business plan—sales, product, marketing, headcount—all must fit together. The FP&A team has to work with functional leaders to model decisions and make tradeoffs. And leaders now have to monitor the plan. They need metrics and early-warning indicators to know if the business is on or off track. In the early days, FP&A is small and helps build the plan. In Sustainability, FP&A becomes mission-critical and must be connected deeply to the company's month-to-month operations.

2. **Sales Ops and Forecasting:** Sales operations and forecasting becomes the core musculature on which the company's revenue plan depends. In the GTM Acceleration and Sustainability stages of Thrival, sales operations 2.0 is very different and strategic.

   Sales Ops 1.0 [Survival] Administrative

   > Compensation and quota plans
   >
   > Salesforce.com/CRM administration
   >
   > Weekly and quarterly forecasting

   Sales Ops 2.0 [Thrival] Strategic & Essential

   > Company growth model & decisions: Model top-line sales targets and an underlying sales and marketing resource plan and expenses to accomplish.

Multiple GTM architecture: Design and execute overall sales architecture, playbooks, supporting team structures, resources, and compensation plans.

Deep metrics & sales efficiency: Deep metrics measure efficiency, validate the sales model, and indicate if company is on or off track.

Enablement: Enabling a global team of sales and channels to be effective.

Forecasting: Not just forecasting for the current quarter, but forecasting for multiple future quarters.

Keep this in mind, however: FP&A and Sales Ops are important, but they operate in conjunction with solid go-to-market leadership to drive execution.

Mindset shift: Clear path to cash flow break-even

The most fundamental aspects of a sustainable business are positive cash flow and profitability. During GTM Acceleration, investors will give startups a hall pass on positive cash flow and profitability, because they believe that investing in rapid customer acquisition and category leadership will pay off in the long run. But in the Sustainability stage the company must "grow up": it has to show continued growth and *simultaneously* demonstrate that it is on a clear path to cash flow and profitability within a specific timeframe.

Tradeoffs become more difficult. Deciding whether to add sales teams or marketing programs becomes a meticulous analytical exercise; the answer is no longer simply "do both." Ratcheting up research and development (R&D) expenses and making strategic acquisitions allow you to enter adjacent markets and cement category leadership, but doing these things increases expenses and pushes out the cash flow break-even date. Operationalization and planning are critical to Sustainability, but they take longer. Operational excellence comes at the expense of speed; decisions and action slow down. These constraints and tradeoffs are all normal, but adjusting to them will be painful for the team. A clear plan, intense discussions, and a good dose of business judgment will help.

Helpful Model: Link revenue generators to expenses. Getting to cash flow break-even is challenging and involves numerous intertwined variables that make it difficult to conceptualize. A helpful model is to link revenue generators to related expense categories, as shown below:

Relate new sales to GTM expenses	Compare the ratio of **new sales contribution** to **GTM expenses** to get the "magic number." $$\frac{\$ \text{ New Billings} \times \text{Gross Margin \%}}{(\$ \text{ Sales Marketing Expense})} = \text{"Magic Number"}$$ *How this helps:* If the ratio is at 1.0 or above, new sales are contributing more than the expenses, which generates positive cash flow. This means GTM is working well! The company may want to invest even more in GTM expenses to drive more growth. The company may deliberately keep the number below 1.0 in some cases where new customers have very high long-term value. If GTM productivity is below 1.0 and customer long-term value is low, then investing in sales and marketing does not drive long-term cash flow break-even, in which case a more fundamental fix to the business is required.
Relate renewal sales to product and customer-support expenses	Compare the **renewals contribution** (renewals multiplied by gross margin percentage) to **non-GTM expenses** (product development, customer success, G&A expense). Think of these as somewhat "fixed costs" that are related to product delivery and customers. *How this helps:* The renewals crossover point (i.e., when the renewal contribution exceeds the non-GTM expenses) is a major milestone and presages cash flow break-even. It's usually easy to predict that point a year in advance. After the renewals crossover milestone, the company may use excess billings from renewals to fund additional GTM growth, industry-leadership initiatives, or drop to the bottom line as cash.

Separating the business into these two threads helps make decisions as to how much to invest where, when to invest, and how to measure progress against the critical business goal of cash flow break-even.

Accelerating cash-burn to achieve cash flow break-even faster. This sounds counterintuitive, but it's possible. If the GTM productivity and renewal rates are good enough—and billings grow faster than R&D expenses—then companies will reach the renewal cross-over point quickly and become cash flow positive at a much larger number. In that case, the company should aggressively fund GTM Acceleration, despite the higher near-term losses. This is the financial basis of a fast GTM Acceleration strategy.

Mindset shift: Drive efficiency and maximize net LTV

During GTM Acceleration, the focus is on top-line growth and managing cash-burn. Shifting into the Sustainability stage changes the focus to what's going on inside the business. Efficiency metrics, unit-cost economics, net LTV models—these now become critical to decision-making. And there are lots of decisions to make. How to grow? Where to invest—and de-invest? Which customers to focus on? Which segments to ignore? What marketing initiatives to fund? Which to kill? Which product lines to expand? Which product lines to kill? What can I do now? What can I wait to do later?

Metrics become core: Establishing, tracking, and evolving metrics enables everyone across the business to measure progress and make both big and small decisions. Metrics require precision in internal systems and financial reporting. Designed well, they pick up on nuances that allow companies to better understand business drivers, detect and troubleshoot problems, and fine-tune operations.

However, there is a trap to watch out for: As the business gravitates to metrics, the tendency is to look at the numbers and simply ask, "Are they going in the right or wrong direction?" This often causes decision-makers to draw conclusions without using business judgment to examine what's going on underneath the metric. That's a problem. It is critical to look underneath key metrics to ensure the underlying mechanics represent reality. Metrics can be skewed by changes in measurement or even incentives, leading to drawing the wrong conclusion.

> **Bob:** "During the later stages at MobileIron, we used customer-evaluation starts as a key metric to measure customer engagement and predict future customer sales. One of our marketing leaders dug into the evaluation

metrics and realized that the compensation plan for our Asian inside-sales team caused a massive burst in evaluations that distorted our trend lines. If we had simply looked at the top-line number, we would have drawn a very wrong conclusion."

Efficiency as a measure of success: Tracking business metrics and growth rates is obviously important to measure results. Equally important is the *efficiency* with which the business produces those results. Sales efficiency: investing $1 in sales/marketing drives $X in new sales. R&D efficiency: investing $1 in product development and generating $Y in new sales or increased renewals. Spending $1 to reduce churn, and gaining $Z in renewals. Investors place significant value on efficiency metrics because it answers a critical question: "If we put X millions of dollars of capital into the business, what return can we get?"

During the Sustainability stage, the leadership team must balance growth and efficiency. The efficiency metrics for sales, marketing, and R&D should be part of the top-line goals for the company and for the executives. By focusing on efficiency, leaders can shift the discussion away from budget constraints and instead can make tough decisions about capital allocation based upon a shared understanding of efficiency and its importance to building a sustainable business that generates positive cash flow.

Prune based upon Net LTV: During GTM Acceleration, the company grew customers and sales rapidly. Not all customer segments or product initiatives will prove to have a positive customer Net LTV, however. The shift to Sustainability requires pruning projects based upon projected Net LTV. Pruning could be reducing—or canceling—investments in customer segments, programs, or product initiatives.

Pruning is painful. Customers who bought from you can be left stranded. Employees who stepped up and shouldered huge projects only to find them canceled. Customers who bet on the company can lose trust and create negative echoes in the marketplace. Employees who see last year's priority project canceled can fear embarking on a new project. Pruning becomes an ongoing discipline for sustainable businesses.

Investor shift: Prepare for crossover and public investors

Once a company achieves accelerated growth and demonstrates that it is on a clear path to cash flow and profitability, it opens itself up to a new base of investors: crossover private investors and public investors through an IPO. Public markets have a new level of demands for financial metrics, and a new level of expectations for growth and predictability. Public markets can provide a healthy and nearly endless supply of capital, but they inflict pain should the company stumble.

An IPO is a wonderful milestone but it's not an end or "exit." It's a beginning. At root, an IPO is two things: (1) a series-A round with a new set of investors (the public ones); and (2) a great marketing event for company credibility.

Drive to Sustainability: Culture and people change

The company is now operating on a different scale: sales and engineering teams are larger than the entire company was just a couple years ago. The team is global, with different cultures and operational pockets spread around the world. The business has evolved to multiple product lines and go-to-markets. Many customers around the world have your product in mission-critical uses. The competitive landscape changed to competing toe-toe with large incumbents. Financial markets and investors place different demands. Planning, communicating, executing, and maintaining culture at scale is harder. In order to balance growth and sustainability at scale, the mindset and culture of the team evolves.

Culture coexistence: Growth with planning and optimization

While continuing to drive growth in the business, the need to plan, operationalize, and optimize begins to change the mindset and the culture. The type of people who are hired change. Increased General & Administrative (G&A) and operational hires shore up the operational foundation from the after-effects of aggressive customer and company expansion. Every functional team—sales, marketing, customer success, engineering—add operational and planning hires to enable better planning and measurement. Leadership roles evolve: executive leaders who excelled in the growth stage struggle to operationalize and plan at the new scale. Instead of the go-go driver, the company now also values operational excellence. The top line goals CEO changes to reflect disciplined growth and path to profitability. The company culture shifts to allow coexistence of the growth culture with the planning and operational culture.

Challenge: The shift creates cultural tension. Expect cultural tension between the early employees who pioneered and turbocharged growth with those who are charged with operationalizing and driving an appropriate level predictability. There is no simple answer. Every successful company faces this. Juggling the encourage-risk-taking-ownership-mentality vs. the get-our-operational-ducks-in-a-row can be balanced.

Advice: Set clear mid-term goals that both growers and optimizers unite around. Redefine the metrics of success to no longer be solely focused on growth and winning deals, and openly talk about the tradeoffs. Example goals for this stage could be:

Company goals: Sustainable Industry Leadership	• Cash flow break-even by Q4 2017
	• Top-line growth of X%. Gain share vs. big competitors
	• Upsell and expand customers, measured by expand rate of 1.3x
	• Deliver A, B, C on core product. Launch expansion into adjacent category
	• Customer satisfaction, measured by NPS > 20 and renewal rate > 94%

Catch-22: Predictability vs. agility

Communications and organizational overhead increases at this stage of the company's growth, but planning and operations can reduce agility. Some loss of agility is natural; too much is stifling. Try to keep project teams relatively small. Amazon, a very large company, restricts team size to "two-pizza teams" that are no larger than two pizzas could feed. Watch the creation of artificial layers in the organization where leaders are stacked on top of each other without enough team to justify a manager.

Predictability can drift into rigidity. Senior leadership must deliberately disrupt the status quo on occasion to avoid rigidity. The classic startup move, which you may have very well done yourself, is to disrupt a category leader that loses their agility.

Team changes: Expect them

The shift from GTM Acceleration to Sustainable Industry Leadership is a jarring transition for the entire company. Roles, mindset, skills, execution all change…again. The job of every leader changes. A great deal of leadership change is common during this phase. (See Book Two, *Survival to Thrival: The People Journey*). Scaling an existing business with its focus on Sustainability requires a different mindset and toolset from the rapid iteration and growth mentality often found in early stage teams. The CEO must candidly assess all leaders not for their past contribution, but for their ability to fit the needs of the company in the sustainable leader phase. And at a very human level, after driving accelerated growth, even very good leaders tire out. Everyone across the leadership team, *including the CEO*, needs to look in the mirror to assess if they are the right person for the next phase of the company. Being a leader that builds a company beyond one's own ability to run is, ironically, a very honorable accomplishment. Yet, the changes are hard. And, the changes are required. Ensuring the right leaders in the right roles for the next phase is by far the best thing for the company, the shareholders, and everyone that put their blood, sweat, and tears into transforming the enterprise startup into a meaningful company.

Success means change: Change is hard but healthy

The company has come an *amazingly* long way since its founding. The little enterprise startup struggling to survive found PMF, accelerated its way to category leadership, and has now transcended the category to become a hugely valuable industry leader. The wild success was both exhilarating and fraught with difficulty. Remember the highs. Remember the lows. And remember the one constant: change.

Success means company change. Company changes mean role changes. Role changes mean the people must change along the way. What gets a company from A to B, is different from what gets a company from B to C, which in turn is different from what gets a company from C to D. Everyone across the company must adapt, and in many cases this means unlearning the very things that made the company successful in the early stages. Change is the natural byproduct of growth and success. Change is hard, but it can be anticipated. Be ready. Be prepared. Change is normal. And most of all, change is healthy.

Your startup has achieved the amazing. What began as a small band of passionate founders is now an industry leader manifesting the company mission and creating enormous value. It's every enterprise entrepreneurs dream. Be bold. Be proud. You earned it.

Punchlines:

» Achieving category leadership is a spectacular accomplishment for a startup, but what truly builds long-term value is becoming a Sustainable Industry Leader.

» Sustainable Industry Leadership requires companies to focus on two things at once: creating a sustainably profitable business while also transcending the initial category. Doing both is hard.

» Industry leadership requires a combination of expanding into adjacent categories, expanding from a product to a platform, and adding multiple GTM models to reach new markets—all of which require the company to painfully alter well-developed muscle memory.

» Transcending the initial category also requires a large mindset shift. The company must re-conceptualize both their internal self-image and external image, which can be particularly difficult for those who ruthlessly focused on initial category leadership.

» Driving to Sustainability requires significant execution shifts. Achieving positive cash flow requires tough tradeoffs. Decision-makers now prioritize operational excellence and efficiency along with growth.

» A new class of investors from the public markets, critical to fueling industry leadership, demand predictability and path to profitability.

» Company culture now balances between the growers and the optimizers, which creates tension. Many leaders who succeed in the growth stages will struggle to adapt.

» As an industry leader, the company gains financial and market strength, but often loses agility, creating an ironic innovators dilemma for the once-nimble enterprise startup.

» The transition to sustainable industry leader is not a smooth landing. Industry leadership unleashes a new cycle of changes and turbulence, except the numbers are now a *lot* bigger.

» Leading a scrappy startup fighting to survive to become a thriving industry leader that manifests the mission is every entrepreneurs' dream—and creates enormous value. Be bold!

CHAPTER 6:
SUMMARY THOUGHTS

Enterprise startups aren't sexy. They're not easy to talk about at cocktail parties, and grandparents likely won't understand them. But enterprise technology underlies our whole economy, and every aspect of enterprise technology is going to be reinvented in the coming decade: The entire compute stack and infrastructure is being reinvented. Applications are being built differently. Mobile is the new user front-end. Identity is being transformed. Analytics are freeing data for decisions. Artificial Intelligence is overturning entire industries. The bottom line: in the coming decade, enterprise startups will present entrepreneurs with a trillion-dollar opportunity.

Building an enterprise startup isn't easy. Going from no product, no revenue, no team, and no capital to Sustainable Industry Leadership on the path to $1B in revenues seems a daunting challenge. Daunting, but not impossible. It's the entrepreneurial dream.

Key to success: Anticipate company change

Everyone cheers the growing startup. Yet, growth causes change. Not just once, but each time the company moves into a new stage: strategies change, execution changes, the business changes, mindsets change, and investors change.

Anticipating these changes is key to enterprise-startup success. Ironically, many of the strategies, execution plans and ways of thinking that lead to success in one stage become the very things that hold a company back in the next stage. So *unlearning*—again and again—is vital. Companies that don't recognize this and adapt will lose steam, miss their opportunities, and fade into irrelevancy.

Unlearning is easy to say in theory, but hard to do in reality. Really hard. Unlearning the past stage and anticipating the next is critical to company success. Unlearning also represents a spectacular learning experience for the CEO, the founders, the leadership team, and everyone in the company.

In the beginning: Survival

The goal in the early stages of the enterprise startup is simple: Survival. Survive long enough to figure out product-market fit and get a sense for early go-to-market.

Founding stage

Pick the right co-founders and refine the idea to create "gravity" that attracts good people and smart capital. Rather than starting with technology, start with a customer problem or industry disruption and work backwards to the solution. Enterprise customers don't buy technology for technology's sake.

Product-Market Fit

Consumer PMF is a well-covered topic. But enterprise PMF is different. It requires paying reference customers who use a product and recommend it to others. There's no shortcut here: to find PMF for an enterprise startup, you need to iterate, iterate, and iterate. Be focused, but not myopic. Be open to adjacent problems, even if they seem like a heretical betrayal of the initial Founding Idea. Often, the

customer hotspot that triggers PMF may be an adjacency. And remember: iterating to find PMF will lead to technical debt and team debt. Be prepared.

PMF is a huge accomplishment. Be proud. Be excited. But there's a catch. PMF is *not* sufficient for enterprise growth. Tons of enterprise companies achieve PMF and win their first 20 customers, but growth never materializes. What's missing?

The "missing link": GTM Fit

For enterprise startups, there is a crucial missing link between finding PMF and unlocking growth. Oddly, it didn't even have a name. We call it Go-To-Market Fit. GTM Fit involves three things: a clear GTM model, a GTM playbook that repeatedly finds and wins customers, and has urgency that answers the question "why now?" The process for finding GTM Fit is much like the process for finding PMF: iterate, iterate, iterate on how customers are found and won.

The search for GTM Fit comes with challenges. It strains the company. Stakes and burn go up. Goals become very easy to hit or miss. The transition from a product-led to a balanced product-GTM strategy tests the culture. Legitimate competition often rears its head during the search for GTM Fit, as others begin to see a similar opportunity, which is a sign you're on the right track.

How does a company know it has GTM Fit? The answer is simple: If it has acceleration and momentum. With GTM Fit, the business accelerates out of survival mode and into Thrival mode.

Then, shift to Thrival

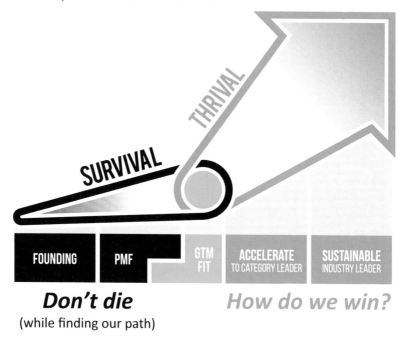

SURVIVAL

THRIVAL

| FOUNDING | PMF | GTM FIT | ACCELERATE TO CATEGORY LEADER | SUSTAINABLE INDUSTRY LEADER |

Don't die
(while finding our path)

How do we win?

Now the mindset changes from "How do we not die?" to "How do we win?" That's Thrival. It's an exhilarating feeling—one of the great moments in the life of an enterprise startup. The startup now has a chance to build a business that creates value and delivers on the mission. A business that *matters*. Savor the feeling.

Within Thrival mode, everything changes—execution, operations, people, culture. Many of the ways of working, thinking, making decisions, and behaving that led to success in the survival phase will now get in the way in the Thrival phase. Much of what used to work won't anymore. The startup must unlearn much of what made it successful. It's maddening, and it's hard, yet it's absolutely crucial to accelerate the business to become a category leader.

Accelerate to Category Leadership

GTM Acceleration is really fun and really scary. The hard questions become: "How fast can we go?" and "When should we slow down?" The startup now has the opportunity to grow fast, separate from the competition, and become a category leader—but at the same time it has to deal with the chaos of acceleration, new operational complexity, drastic changes in everyone's jobs, and the need to unlearn old habits. With each hard-fought success milestone, a new round of change and pain comes into view. Early metrics and operational gauges become critical to holding together a rapidly accelerating company. Execution shifts from stingy survival practices to calculated recklessness. It feels schizophrenic: grow fast to become a category leader, while also laying down the early foundation of the path to a profitable sustainable business.

Sustainable Industry Leadership

The startup is now a fast-growing category leader with significant revenue. Few startups ever achieve this. Now the challenge becomes simultaneously transcending the original startup category to become an overall industry leader while also driving towards profitability and positive cash flow. Everything changes again. Tradeoffs become more disciplined. Operational excellence and efficiency become increasingly important. A new class of investors (often public investors) provide capital through an IPO. And, surprisingly, executive roles and culture change again. Sustainable Industry Leaders truly thrive, transform entire markets, create massive shareholder value—and manifest the mission that catalyzed the startup journey many years before.

Sometimes there isn't a great answer

Many of the situations in which you find yourself as an enterprise entrepreneur have no good or easy answers. It helps to know they are coming, to predict the problems, but in the end that knowledge doesn't make the situation any easier. Do what you have to do and then move on. And know that everyone has their turn in the barrel. You are not alone.

Change is hard but change is healthy

This book covers the challenges and changes that enterprise startups confront and overcome on the journey from passionate founding team to a sustainable industry leader. The changes are hard, humbling, but also a tremendous learning experience.

What's next? As the company changes, every job changes, and so must everyone in the company—from the CEO to the leadership team to every employee. They must change how they work, how they interact, how they lead, and how they behave. The people-specific changes along the enterprise-startup journey can be harder and more dramatic than the company changes. But they're equally necessary and satisfying. The next book, *Survival to Thrival: The People Journey* is about more personal changes and challenges as roles dramatically evolve along the journey from a founding team to an industry leader. The key take away, unsurprisingly, is *unlearning the way to success.*

Celebrate along the way and have fun!

Building a startup from "nothing to something" is excruciatingly hard. Through intense execution, anticipating change, overcoming painful speed bumps, and a good dose of luck, entrepreneurial teams can accomplish the amazing and transform industries.

Celebrate every milestone. Savor every victory. Your journey is an inspiration to us and enterprise entrepreneurs everywhere.

As Ralph Waldo Emerson said:
"Life is a journey, not a destination."

Survive well. Thrive well. Pass it on.

Bob & Tae Hea

NOTES